A Constructed View

A Constructed View
THE ARCHITECTURAL PHOTOGRAPHY
OF JULIUS SHULMAN

JOSEPH ROSA

with an essay by Esther McCoy

RIZZOLI
NEW YORK

To my wife, Louise

Throughout this book, the title and year of the photograph are noted in bold type; its location and any other information in roman type; and the architect, designer, or artist, and year of the work in italic type. All locations are in California unless otherwise specified. All camera sizes are noted in inches.

First published in the United States of America in 1994 by
RIZZOLI INTERNATIONAL PUBLICATIONS, INC.
300 Park Avenue South
New York, New York 10010
www.rizzoliusa.com

ISBN: 978-0-8478-1777-1

Library of Congress Cataloguing-in-Publication Data
Rosa, Joseph
A constructed view: the architectural photography of Julius Shulman / by Joseph Rosa ;
with an essay by Esther McCoy
p. cm.
Includes bibliographical reference and index.
ISBN 978-0-8478-1777-1
1. Architectural photography. 2. Shulman, Julius. I. McCoy, Esther. II. Title.
TR659.R6293   1994
770'.92—dc20   CIP 93-39735

Frontispiece: Julius Shulman in 1982

Design by Kim Shkapich
Printed and bound in Singapore

First published by Rizzoli in 1994, reprinted in 2008

Acknowledgments

Over the years that I have been conducting research on Julius Shulman, numerous individuals have shared their thoughts and memories of him as well as their knowledge of architectural photography in relation to twentieth-century modern architecture. First and foremost, I would like to thank Julius Shulman for opening his home, studio, and life to me. During the course of this project I made many trips to Los Angeles, and I also relocated there for a brief period. Shulman graciously accommodated my visits and interviews and worked tirelessly with me in reviewing his archives. The hospitality and friendship of Olga and Julius Shulman, and his daughter Judy McKee, deserve my warmest gratitude.

Many thanks to Diana I. Agrest, Mardges Bacon, Peter D. Eisenman, Mary McLeod, and Bernard Tschumi for their encouragement, advice, and moral support; to David Gebhard, Thomas S. Hines, and Kurt W. Forster for sharing their knowledge of modernism and the architectural photography of California; and to the Getty Center for the History of Art and the Humanities for my Visiting Scholar status (late spring 1991), which provided me with office and research facilities as well as housing during my brief stay in Los Angeles.

Throughout this research I have interviewed and corresponded with numerous individuals to whom I am indebted: Janet Abrams, Ilse Bing, Marc Dessauce, Albert Frey, Elizabeth Gordon, Bill Hedrich, Philip Johnson, Edward Killingsworth, Pierre Koenig, Norman McGrath, Hildegard Frank Ober, Marvin Rand, Terence Riley, Cervin Robinson, Naomi Sawelson-Gorse, Woody Siegel, and Ezra Stoller.

Institutions and individuals who have assisted me in my research include Tony P. Wrenn and Pam Meehan of the American Institute of Architects Library and Archives, Washington, D.C.; Andrew Mead of the Architectural Press, *Architects' Journal*, London, England; the library staff at the Avery Architectural and Fine Arts Library, Columbia University, New York; Louise Desy and Suzelle Baudouin of the Ilse Bing Papers, Photographic Collection, Canadian Centre for Architecture, Montreal; Carolyn Davis of the Margaret Bourke-White Papers, Department of Special Collections, Syracuse University Library; the Cultural Heritage Board, Los Angeles; Tod Justavson of the George Eastman House, Rochester, New York; the library staff at the Getty Center's Resource Collection, Los Angeles; Anne Champagne of the F. S. Lincoln Collection, Rare Books Room, the University Libraries, Pennsylvania State University; Barbara J. Dawson of the Esther McCoy Papers, Archives of American Art, Washington, D.C.; Lloyd Morgan of the Willard & Barbara Morgan Archives, Morgan & Morgan Press, Dobbs Ferry, New York; Jennifer Brody in the Department of Architecture and Design and Lisa Archambeau in the Registrar's Archive, The Museum of Modern Art, New York; Ann Caiger of the Richard J. Neutra Collection, Department of Special Collections at the library of the University of California, Los Angeles; and Wendy Car of the Raphael Soriano Papers, ENV Archives, California State Polytechnic University, Pomona.

I am also grateful to David Morton, my editor at Rizzoli, for supporting the project; to associate editor Andrea Monfried; and to Kim Shkapich for understanding Shulman's photographic "eye" and designing a book that beautifully illustrates it.

Finally, special thanks to my wife, Louise Lavenstein Rosa, who has patiently assisted me on this book from its inception to the final manuscript.

Joseph Rosa
New York, 1993

1

Figure 1
Sunday Trekkers on Mount
Hollywood, 1933

Figure 2
Raphael Soriano and
Basque Shepherd, 1936

2

PERSISTENCE OF VISION

Julius Shulman was born with that rare eye that sees. This gift of perception was enhanced when his family moved from Brooklyn, where he was born in 1910, to a small farm in Connecticut. Subtle changes of light were more significant in the country, and dozens of gradations from sunrise to dusk informed his sensitive eye. As a child, he discovered nature with a capital N—so strong that it was to become a major force both in his life and his photography.

When he was ten, his family moved to California, presenting him with a new set of visual changes. One was the quickness between sunset and dark. Shulman's earliest photographs demonstrated his perceptive eye—a particular picture of an all-city high school track meet at the Los Angeles Coliseum, taken with a Brownie box camera at age seventeen, revealed a mastery of movement as well as perspective and framing *(fig. 3, page 37)*. A mere teenager, but his eye could compose.

His shot of Sunday hikers resting at the crest of Mount Hollywood is a wonderful photographic cartoon *(fig. 1)*. Fifty years before smart jogger suits, Shulman showed the Depression athlete in clothes ready for the ragbag. The hikers look out across the San Fernando Valley, then only lightly sprinkled with houses.

He came by chance to architectural photography. A Richard Neutra draftsman who rented a room from Shulman's sister took him to see Neutra's Kun House off Hollywood Boulevard. Shulman's vest-pocket Kodak shots of it so pleased Neutra that he asked him to photograph other work. Under Neutra's strict guidance, Shulman graduated to a view camera, and his career as one of the great documenters of the built environment began in earnest. His start coincided with a period of pronounced creativity in architecture. Shulman photographed for such important L.A. architects as R. M. Schindler, Raphael Soriano, Gregory Ain, and Harwell Harris.

His only guidance aside from Neutra's were some pointers in "dynamic symmetry" (which he had been practicing intuitively) from a cousin, an art teacher in Detroit. He studied seven years at UCLA and Berkeley, but his major concern was always light—the medium by which the feeling of a building is transmitted.

What Shulman remembers most vividly about his self-education in photography he recounts in images as vivid as any he made on film. He recalls how he printed postcards of his photographs and put them for sale in a bookstore while at Berkeley. His faith in himself was rewarded by the steady demand. Photography, he discovered, could be more than a pastime.

His mother encouraged him as a child to eat raw vegetables, and he became an early health-food faddist, crunching on raw carrots as he strode the Hollywood Hills. His love of nature, which enveloped him in childhood, would mature in the 1950s into a herculean program of terracing the slope behind his house above Laurel Canyon, now the site of hundreds of species of plants.

It was through Shulman that the message of California reached the eastern editors. Before him, the message rarely got beyond the Rockies before it was blown back. He carried his photographs to the editors in the East and had a great deal to do with educating them about what to see in western design.

As a writer, I had worked with other photographers before Shulman, but none was as decisive. We walked around the site together, talking about the design of the house—the massing, the volumes, the orientation.

Shulman would break in with "a two o'clock shot," and we would move along. Later on he'd say, "I'll take this at sunset to get the last light on that wall," or "This will work in a four o'clock sun." After an hour spent turning the house into a sundial, he'd say, "Well, shall we go to lunch?"

I was shocked that he could leave so soon. But when we returned, he found the exact spots and pointed the camera in the direction his eye had recommended for that hour. Sometimes he would move the camera a foot over, but usually his initial quick preliminary decision was right on the button. He always got the essential facts from that first walk around—the house against the trees, the reflections on the glass, the roofline against the clouds. He loved a dramatic sky. His eye, which gathered so quickly, retained the image he wanted. Rarely did he have to go back for more shots. His incisive vision had deftly encompassed the design.

No other photographer had ever invited me to participate in the work. With our heads together under the black cloth, our eyes fixed on the ground glass, he'd call to his assistant to turn an Eames chair fifteen degrees to the right, or to replace a vase of flowers on the coffee table with a small Natzler bowl, or to twist the potted philodendron so that only one large leaf extended into the frame of the photograph. After the first time, we always read the ground glass together whenever we worked on an assignment. But once when I asked him what f-stop to use for a certain shot, he brushed the question aside: "That's not important. You can learn that anywhere. Learning to see is the important thing."

He was the only photographer I knew who placed people in architectural photographs. "Witnesses," nineteenth-century architects called the people they drew in perspective drawings to give scale to the buildings. I stood in for scale in many a Shulman photograph.

There is one famous photograph of Shulman's that uses a witness for a different purpose. It is the twilight shot of Neutra's Palm Springs Kaufmann House, a forty-five-minute exposure in which the light was introduced to define the swimming pool, then, with the camera turned off, the witness (Mrs. Kaufmann) took her place on a pad beside the pool to screen the light *(fig. 49, page 75)*. But Shulman's mainstay was not clever tricks: it was an eye that knew how light blessed a building.

In his studio, across the court from his house in the Hollywood Hills, are archives of fifty-some years of work in the cause of architecture. Both the house and studio are Cultural Heritage Board monuments. The buildings are steel-framed pavilions designed by Raphael Soriano and built in the same period as Soriano's Case Study House, which was part of the recent Museum of Contemporary Art show. Shulman's tender photograph of Soriano in the thirties shows him with a Basque shepherd they met on a hike in the hills above East L.A., after Soriano's exuberance had won over the flinty shepherd and his dogs *(fig. 2)*.

Shulman lives with his wife, Olga, in the Soriano house and studio. His planting program to stabilize the adjacent slope was disrupted by a 1952 rockslide after a monumental rain. Pinned by the slide, he came out with a broken leg; in a cast, he directed the terracing of the hillside. Today the redwoods he planted are seventy-five feet tall. Gardening, backpacking, and skiing remain favorite activities.

His reputation as a California architectural photographer was made early, but after a few years the subjects encompassed many parts of the United States and other continents. His two books on photography, *Photography of Architecture and Interiors* and *Photography of Architecture and Design,* are standards for the state of the art. But he has been a consultant on two dozen other books, the latest, *Steps and Stairways.*

Today, Shulman is not about to retire; indeed, he is busier than ever. There are too many visitors to his files, all happy to reminisce with the photographer who saw it all happen and can put his hand on any negative in five minutes at most. He can give you twice the time in memories of the architect, the building, and the particular year the photograph was shot.

Southern California architecture was first known outside the state largely due to Shulman's industry. Now the wind blows to the West. Voted an honorary fellow by the AIA and recipient of its gold medal for architectural photography, he enjoys the international esteem of a new generation eager for images of the past to inform present and future. In capturing the vision of so many others, Shulman's eye has ultimately defined his own vision, which remains as keen and singular as the man himself.

Esther McCoy
Los Angeles, 1989

This essay, originally titled "Persistence of Vision: The Encompassing Eye of Architectural Photographer Julius Shulman," was first published in the March 1990 issue of *Angeles.* It was the last article Esther McCoy wrote for publication before her death on December 30, 1989.

2

1. Architectural Nude, 1952

2. Glass Discs, 1938

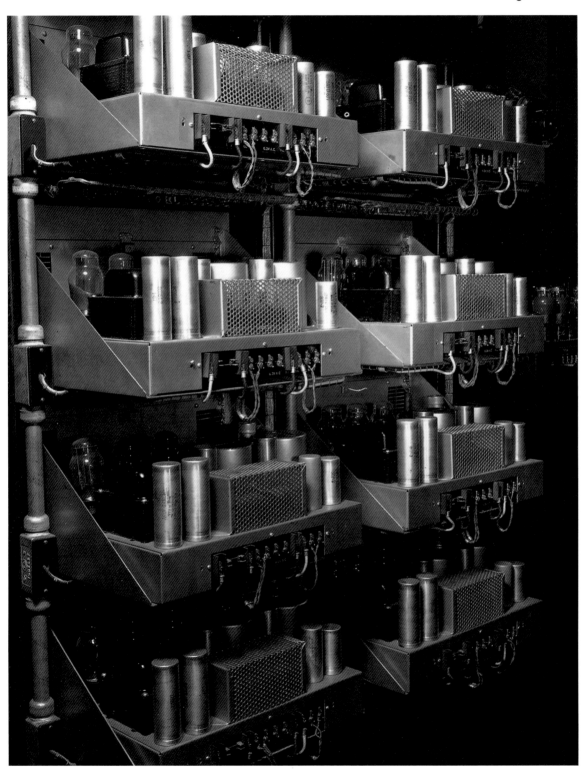

4

3. NBC Transmitter, 1938

4. Shulman House and
Studio under construction,
1949, Los Angeles, *Raphael
Soriano, 1950*

5. Strathmore Apartments, 1939, Los Angeles, *Richard Neutra, 1937*

6. Harris House, 1942, Los Angeles, *R. M. Schindler, 1942*

5

6

"Does the photographer
or the architect
anticipate
what is being resolved during an exposure?"

Walter Gropius, 1963

7

7. CBS Television City, 1953, Los Angeles, *Pereira and Luckman, 1952*

8–10. Case Study House #21, 1958, Los Angeles, *Pierre Koenig, 1958*

9

10

11

12

11, 12. Malin "Chemo-
sphere" House, 1960, Los
Angeles, *John Lautner, 1960*

13

13. Smalley House, 1974, Beverly Hills, *A. Quincy Jones, 1973*

14–17. Case Study House #8 (Eames House), 1950 (black and white), 1958 (color), *Pacific Palisades, Ray and Charles Eames, 1949*

16

17

18

18. Ocho Cascades, 1980,
Puerto Vallarta, Mexico,
Edward Giddings, ca. 1980

19. Shelton House, 1979,
Bel Air, *Charles Moore,
1978*

19

20

20, 21. Lovell "Health"
House, 1950, Los Angeles,
Richard Neutra, 1929

21

22

22. IBM Facility, 1981,
Mexico City, Mexico,
Ricardo Legorreta, 1977

23. Lever House, 1959,
New York, New York,
Skidmore, Owings &
Merrill, 1952

25

24. Seagram Building, 1958,
New York, New York,
Mies van der Rohe with
Philip Johnson, 1958

25. Lake Shore Drive Apart-
ments, 1958, Chicago,
Illinois, *Mies van der Rohe,*
1951

A Constructed View
The Architectural Photography of Julius Shulman

Architectural photography—or better, architecture through photography—shares some ground with surrealist photography, if not with surrealism, in that particular quality of the ready-made and of the grouping of photographs of buildings and places to create a repertory of found objects. In the photography of architecture is the potential for that moment of silence when everything disappears and we enter another world . . . where a sentimental relationship is established with the image, "framed like a caged bird," and where places become "inhabitable rather than visible."

—Diana Agrest, "Framework for a Discourse on Representation," *Places and Memories*

A Brief History

Julius Shulman was born, the fourth of Max (1878–1923) and Yetta (1886–1975) Shulman's five children, on October 10, 1910, in Brooklyn, New York. Shulman's parents were Russian Jews who as young children had immigrated to the United States with their parents. Both of their families took up residence in Brooklyn, where Max and Yetta eventually met and married. Four months after Julius was born, the family moved to Connecticut, living in various locations before finally settling in Central Village in 1914. Here his parents purchased a one-hundred-acre farm with livestock, which they operated successfully to support the family. Also, shortly after acquiring the farm, Max established a small fur business, purchasing pelts from as far afield as northern Maine and Canada, and selling them to furriers from New York City. Julius vividly remembers his father as an "energetic man, always on the go." So it is not surprising that the pioneer spirit ultimately drew Max to California, which was for him "the land of gold and oranges"; his family stayed in Connecticut while he set about establishing a new business in Los Angeles.[1]

By 1920, Max had started a dry goods store and was able to buy a small two-story house for his family; at this time he was rejoined by Yetta, Julius, then ten, and his siblings, who had crossed the country via train. Upon arrival in California, the Shulmans settled in Boyle Heights, East Los Angeles, one of the first Jewish communities in Southern California (and also the location of the family business). Only three years later, when Julius was thirteen, his father died of tuberculosis, having literally worked himself to death. This left Yetta alone to raise their five children, keep house, and manage the store.

Julius was the only sibling who seldom worked in the family business; instead he went on to attend college. He attributes this to his mother's insight and the absence of his "disciplinarian" father, as he says she encouraged her son to do what he wanted with his life.[2] In addition, he was by this time immersed in the outdoor life, having spent his formative years roaming the farm in Connecticut; he had also become a very active member of the Boy Scouts the year before his father died.[3]

Shulman's introduction to and only formal training in photography was an elective art course at Roosevelt High School in Los Angeles when he was sixteen—there he learned the basics. Shulman's Track Meet photograph of 1927 *(fig. 3)* was taken with his family's Brownie box camera, and it earned him an A in the class.[4] Although the photograph was taken by a young novice who had just learned to use a camera *(fig. 4)*, it shows the genesis of Shulman's capacity to compose a striking photograph.

Figure 3
Track Meet, 1927

Figure 4
Julius Shulman in 1927

Figure 5
Windblown Tree, 1934,
Berkeley

3

4

5

Fortunately, the stock market crash of 1929 did not have a catastrophic effect on the Shulman family business, thus allowing Julius to enter the University of California at Los Angeles's School of Engineering that same year. After the first two weeks of classes he decided not to continue in the engineering program, but instead to audit courses for the rest of his five years at the college, in pursuit of a major that would truly interest him. Based on his inherent love of nature and the outdoors, he considered becoming a geologist or even a forest ranger, but his curiosity subsided when he realized that chemistry would be a requirement.[5]

For pleasure, Shulman continued to photograph, first with his Brownie box camera, then from 1931 until 1933 with a 2¼ x 3¼ camera he purchased, and then with a Kodak vest-pocket camera he received as a birthday gift.[6] His photographs from 1933 and 1934 illustrate the vast territory that he would travel to discover compositions. Either by himself or with a friend who also enjoyed photography, he would "wander around the beaches and the Santa Monica Mountains to hike and take pictures."[7] The photographs taken at this time document various landscapes and structures of the California coastal regions. In photographs from Shulman's 1933 view of Al's Market in Los Angeles (fig. 7) to his 1934 portrayals of the Ford Building at the San Diego International Exposition (fig. 8) and of a tree in the Berkeley Hills (fig. 5), different aspects of photographic depiction are addressed, from straight to pictorial photography. Shulman was a pluralist when it came to subject matter as well. His ability was publicly recognized at this time: in 1933, his photograph Sixth Street Bridge (fig. 6) won the first prize in a competition sponsored by an East Coast–based magazine. The judge was famed photojournalist Margaret Bourke-White.[8]

In Shulman's fifth year of auditing courses at UCLA, a friend who was moving to attend the University of California at Berkeley suggested that he look into what that college might have to offer. From spring 1934 through fall 1935 Shulman continued his studies at Berkeley. Between classes he wandered around the campus with his vest-pocket camera, taking photographs of several of the buildings. Later in the evenings, he would develop the photographs with a small enlarger that he had brought with him from Los Angeles. Soon, friends who saw these photographs barraged him with requests, asking him to sell copies at the local and campus bookstores. Shulman realized that it would be a way to earn some money while in school, and so he started making multiple 8 x 10 prints, framing them, and selling them on campus. This led to requests for portraits from students in the drama department. Julius enjoyed taking the photographs and did not consider himself a "photographer" at this time, nor did he think of becoming a professional.[9]

Figure 6
Sixth Street Bridge, 1933,
Los Angeles

Figure 7
Al's Market, 1933,
Los Angeles

6

39

Figure 8
Ford Building, 1934,
San Diego International
Exposition

Figure 9
Phoebe Apperson Hearst
Memorial Gymnasium for
Women, 1934, University
of California, Berkeley,
Bernard Maybeck and
Julia Morgan, 1925

Figure 10
Life Sciences Building, 1934,
University of California,
Berkeley

Figure 11
Campanile, 1934,
University of California,
Berkeley

9

10

11

The notion of "framing" the subject matter becomes more evident in Shulman's 1934 photographs of the Berkeley campus. These include a literal framed view through a window in the Campanile *(fig. 11)* and an implied frame of objects in the foregrounds of photographs of the Life Sciences Building *(fig. 10)* and the Phoebe Apperson Hearst Memorial Gymnasium for Women *(fig. 9)*. All of these photographs are asymmetrical in composition and depict fragments of buildings and landscape that embody a visual aura of the campus setting. Shulman maintains that he never learned technique—"it was a hit-or-miss process"—but the ability to compose the frame of the photograph had become second nature.[10]

Shulman returned to Los Angeles from Berkeley in February 1936. Shortly after this he became friends with a young man who was working for the architect Richard Neutra.[11] Shulman met this man through his sister Shirley, who was renting him a room in her house. Shirley lived in the Silverlake area, where she owned a drugstore; the Neutras also happened to live in this community and frequented her store.[12] At the end of February, Shulman received an impromptu invitation to accompany his friend on an inspection of Neutra's Kun House, which was under construction at the time. He brought along his vest-pocket camera (and a tripod) and meandered about the property, taking roughly half a dozen photographs of the house in its Los Angeles landscape context *(figs. 12, 13)*. Shulman made prints that week and gave a set to his friend. By Saturday of the same week, his friend called to tell him that Neutra had seen the pictures and wanted an interview. Consequently, on March 5, Shulman went to meet Neutra at his office in Silverlake; this meeting was perhaps the most significant turning point in Shulman's life.

Figures 12, 13
Kun House, 1936,
Los Angeles,
Richard Neutra, 1936

One of the first things Neutra asked Shulman was whether he was a professional architectural photographer, and Shulman informed Neutra that he was not. After they had discussed Shulman's background and interest in photography, Neutra asked to purchase Shulman's Kun House photographs and also whether he would be interested in photographing other works. Shulman accepted and was given a list of projects to view. Neutra also told Shulman to go meet Raphael Soriano, a young man who had worked for him and was just finishing his first building, the Lipetz House in the Silverlake area. After his meeting with Neutra, Shulman drove over and introduced himself to Soriano, who was at the site, and began to photograph for Soriano as well.[13] Neutra's decision to purchase Shulman's photographs helped to establish him firmly as a professional photographer in the architectural community, and in the ensuing weeks, Neutra introduced Shulman to such influential and progressive architects as R. M. Schindler, Gregory Ain, and J. R. Davidson. Thus, by the end of 1936 Shulman's logbook of photo assignments read as a *Who's Who* of Southern California architects.[14]

12

43

From 1936 until 1943, when Shulman entered the army, he received a constant flow of photography commissions, and he worked out of his apartment. His bathroom doubled as a darkroom until 1937, when he married Emma Romm and set up a small freestanding shed in his backyard instead.[15] During these early years Shulman had no assistance, and he set up the composition and auxiliary lighting for his assignments and processed his own prints. However, this was to his advantage, as he concurrently received an education in modern architecture: "A photographic session of one or two days allowed for extensive analyses of compositions and design elements. There was also time for a true educational process." In these early years many architects and designers did not have overwhelming amounts of work, so they would attend the sessions with Shulman. He says that those days were most rewarding in terms of "the exchange of discussion regarding design composition and evaluation of spatial relationships."[16]

Occasionally Shulman also did portraits for advertisements *(fig. 14)* as well as product and furniture photographs for designers such as Walter Dorwin Teague *(figs. 15, 16)*, Paul T. Frankel *(fig. 17)*, Paul Laszlo, and Raymond Loewy. In many ways he was a successful photographer and businessman before he was even aware of the fact. For the seven years he was in practice prior to going off to war, he was very active photographing buildings and producing reprints for architects and publications. But it wasn't until 1941, when Shulman photographed the Shangri-La Apartments by William Foster *(fig. 18)*, and was given a large order for prints from the hotel's furniture manufacturer (the Los Angeles Furniture Company), that he realized he was truly established. He also realized that another market could be explored—the reprints of photographs for manufacturers.[17]

Shulman entered the army in October 1943; he was assigned the position of army hospital photographer at Baxter General Hospital in Spokane, Washington. Most of his time in the army was spent in surgery, photographing procedures for medical reports. When Julius left for the army, Emma was expecting their first child and moved in with her mother.[18] Their daughter, Judy, was born in April 1944. Shulman returned from the army in October 1945 and moved in with his daughter and Emma at her mother's house.[19] Reimmersing himself in architectural photography, he rented an apartment at Sixth and Western in Los Angeles and converted it into an office. Shulman's office remained at this location until the construction of his and Emma's house and studio in Laurel Canyon (designed by Soriano) was completed in 1950. The new studio signified an important change in Shulman's professional career; he no longer did his own printing but hired a small staff which included an assistant and an in-house printer. As Shulman's volume of work continuously grew, it became essential that someone else produce the prints.

Figure 14
Brassiere Advertisement,
1937

Figure 15
Scott Radio, 1937,
Walter Dorwin Teague

Figure 16
Schlage Hardware, 1937,
Walter Dorwin Teague

Figure 17
Frankel Gallery, 1942,
Beverly Hills,
Paul T. Frankel, ca. 1940

14

15

16

17

18

This was carried out under Shulman's direction, as a significant aspect of Shulman's photography evolves during darkroom manipulation. That Shulman no longer printed his own photographs is of important note. Besides the ever growing number of commissions, a vast quantity of reprints was constantly being requested by magazines and architects. Shulman reflects, "The amount of reprints we continually got just from Richard [Neutra] could keep one person busy for months." The office became, in a sense, a second family, with his wife taking care of the paperwork for almost two decades. From 1950 until Shulman's retirement in 1986 his studio functioned in this manner.[20]

Shulman acknowledges that "photographing modern architecture for Neutra was a rare start." From 1936 to 1968 Shulman documented over 90 percent of Neutra's buildings.[21] Before Neutra commissioned Shulman, most of his buildings were photographed by Luckhaus Studios, with a smaller body of work documented by Willard D. Morgan.[22] Most of these photographs do not reveal the buildings as machines in the American landscape but instead have a closer affiliation to the visual imagery of many other "modern" houses built in Europe.[23] Neutra, in fact, became an architectural hero in Europe partially because he was building in America. The avant-garde aesthetic he was using had already been institutionalized abroad, but was still relatively new in the United States.[24]

Shulman provided Neutra with the visual difference he needed to represent his works. Shulman's photographs were mostly perspectival in composition, framing the buildings within their landscape. Another reason his photographs were better suited to represent Neutra's works was Shulman's practice of over-exposing the film to achieve shade intensity (which he countered by reducing developing time). This allowed the contrast of the photograph's shade and shadow to read more dramatically and to bring out the tonal value of the sky. This aspect is evident even in Shulman's earliest photographs, where shadow is just as important as subject matter *(figs. 19, 20)*.

Neutra was well aware of the problems that could occur with photographs that did not contextualize his architecture. He was the only architect contributing to "Modern Architecture—International Exhibition" at The Museum of Modern Art in 1932 (curated by Henry-Russell Hitchcock and Philip Johnson) who was asked to have one of his buildings (the Lovell House) rephotographed to show more mature vegetation.[25]

Clearly Neutra realized the latent talent and potential of the young novice. In a letter to Shulman, Neutra's wife, Dione, reflects on their years of collaboration: "Richard never fails to speak with delight of how 'his' [buildings] through 'your' [photographs have] . . . worked the best!"[26] Shulman's photographs

19

20

created the "American image" that Neutra needed to present to Europe through magazines and books. Many of Neutra's later publications consist of Shulman's "photographs looking 'out from' houses rather than 'at' them . . . showing off some of the nation's finest scenery."[27] His photographs illustrated Neutra's ideology, expressed the use of materials, and at times provided the ideal image of the material. During the early years many of the houses had steel window frames with entrance and garage doors constructed of wood instead of metal and painted silver to simulate the image of the machine-made. This worked very well for the camera lens; the painted surface read as silver, further enhancing and perpetuating the Neutra image. Neutra understood the importance of establishing iconographic images of his architecture to represent his ideology. In a letter reflecting on Shulman's photography, Neutra states, "His work will survive me. Film [is] stronger and good glossy prints are easier [to] ship than brute concrete, stainless steel, or even ideas."[28]

Figure 19
Woman with Shadow,
1933, Newport Beach

Figure 20
Sand Dune Detail, 1938,
Death Valley

Shulman and Neutra's relationship was an idiosyncratic one *(fig. 21)*. Their mutual concern for the most informative views allowed Shulman to absorb the qualities of modern architecture, and in turn his inherent ability to compose a photograph presented Neutra's buildings to the world as no one else could. In the early years Neutra directed a large number of the assignments, from the views through to the camera angle; this was a good though exasperating experience for Shulman. But over time, they reached an understanding that allowed Shulman more creative freedom.[29] Neutra once described their early working relationship thus: "[We] may have fought a little and agreed much less than in our later years of cooperation . . . too bad life is so short."[30] Over the years Shulman's visits to Neutra became a ritual they both grew to enjoy. Shulman would arrive in the evening hours with prints from his most recent assignment; Neutra would usually be resting in his bedroom. They would then spend hours reviewing prints for master file sets. Shulman knew that Neutra looked forward to the evening visits; Neutra often remarked on how much he had learned about his own design through the photographs.[31]

Shulman took it for granted that "furniture readjusting" would be required on a Neutra assignment. Usually the photo session would take place when the owner was not at home. "Neutra would arrive with two men from his office and a few selected pieces of furniture of his own design and a carpet or two." The two men would remove the furniture Richard did not want in the photo; this sometimes included the draperies if they disrupted the interior-exterior relationship of the house with the landscape. Shulman recalls, "Neutra was adamant about removing what he called 'bad furniture' from his homes' photographs."[32]

21

22

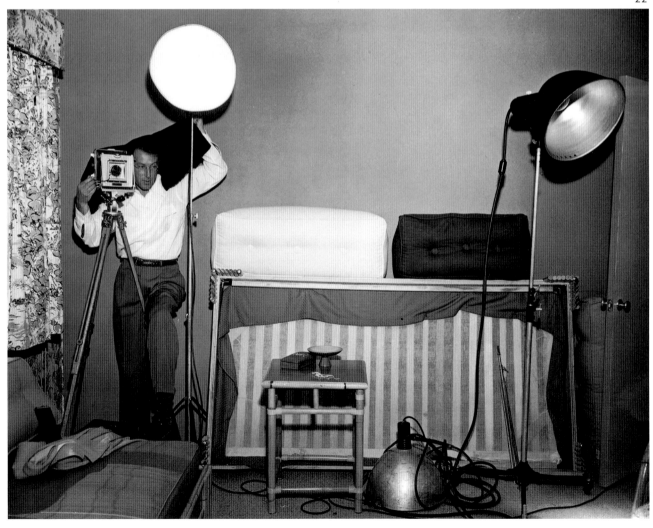

The architectural historian Esther McCoy was well aware of the architect's and photographer's role in modifying interiors to create the recorded image. In her essay "The Important House," published in *The New Yorker* in April 1948, McCoy elegantly illustrates the relationship between a fictional, world-renowned architect and a photographer. The inspiration for the article came during a magazine assignment Shulman did with McCoy of a house.[33] A photograph from the shoot depicts Shulman in the corner of a room with unwanted furniture stacked up against the wall to remove it from the frame of the camera *(fig. 22)*. Although this particular house was not designed by Neutra, McCoy modeled her fictional characters on Neutra and Shulman. The essay reveals the elaborate preparation necessary to make a photograph, as well as the confusion felt by the typical homeowner trying to differentiate between the home the family occupied and the ideal home the magazine would depict. On another level, McCoy illustrates how the role of the photographer in the creation of the architect's image was typically perceived as marginal, as throughout the text the architect is referred to as Mr. Aidan, while the photographer is never mentioned by name:

> The photographer was moving the garden furniture. He picked up some new metal chairs and carried them around to the enclosed drying yard. . . . "What's wrong with the new chairs?" Mrs. Blakeley asked him. "They were a little high," the photographer answered. . . . She [then] heard Mr. Aidan and the photographer talking to [her neighbor]. A few minutes later, they came back carrying two chairs and a low, glass-topped table. They set them on the terrace . . . [and] the photographer tried them out in various positions. . . . Then she heard them come into the house and start moving some things in the living room. After a while she went back into the living room . . . [and] noticed with a shudder that the couch was missing. In its place was a cot from the sun deck, just a metal tube frame with a gray canvas mattress.

Shulman specifically remembers one instance in which he was dismayed by Neutra's process of "readjusting the furniture"—the assignment to photograph the Maslon House at the Tamarisk Country Club in Cathedral City in 1963:

> Neutra's concept of a house is an empty one. So when we photographed the Maslon House, he took out all the art and most of the furniture. Never before had I been so offended! Mrs. Maslon granted my request, and two weeks later I went back and photographed the house the way she lived in it. It was published in *Connaissance des Arts,* but Neutra never commented about the publication. [Perhaps he] never realized that I had rephotographed the house.[34]

This was the only time Shulman ever rephotographed a Neutra house without the architect's prior knowledge. In rephotographing this residence, Shulman insured the same visual frame, thus providing a rare opportunity to compare the way Neutra intended his dwelling to be depicted with the way the home was actually used. In the earlier photograph *(fig. 23)* the open living-dining area is sparsely furnished and not recognizable as such an area. The later photograph *(fig.24)* depicts furnishings disposed in a manner that showed the open space as having its different functions.

Shulman's disapproval of Neutra's austere interior aesthetics was evident when he chose not to have the architect design his and Emma's house and studio in Laurel Canyon. When, in 1948, Shulman commissioned Raphael Soriano instead, many friends, including certain magazine editors, wondered why. Neutra had, after all, launched Shulman's career as a professional photographer. Having worked so closely with Neutra for almost ten years, Shulman realized that "Neutra would do what Neutra wanted, not necessarily want I wanted or needed." He therefore decided not to commission Neutra, having known the man from the myth and the reality from the photograph.[35]

As Shulman and Soriano were very good friends and saw eye to eye, Soriano encouraged him to contribute his own ideas toward his and Emma's new home (something Neutra would never have allowed). Shulman's specific requests included the screened porches which anchor the house to the site, the studio, and the kitchen layout; "a proper working kitchen" was one aspect of design at which Shulman did not think Soriano was terribly successful.[36] The only other architect Shulman had considered for the job was R. M. Schindler. Shulman had photographed some of Schindler's buildings as early as 1936, knew him socially, and "thought [he] could live with his architecture." Shulman and Neutra never discussed the fact that Soriano received the commission.[37]

Although Neutra was a good architect, he was an even better publicist.[38] Throughout his career Neutra did all of his own promotional work; Shulman rarely publicized Neutra's work as he did for many other clients.[39] However, through his photographs of Neutra's buildings Shulman became known to a vast array of consumer- and trade-magazine editors, and in the ensuing years Shulman was hired by many of these editors to do photo assignments for their publications. During these decades Shulman's status at many of these magazines was that of a photographic consultant or staff photographer.[40]

One of Shulman's earliest and most notable working relationships with magazines began with *Arts & Architecture,* then owned and edited by John Entenza. Shulman started doing assignments for Entenza in 1938, shortly after the latter had purchased the magazine (then titled *California Arts & Architecture*). By December 1942 Shulman's name started to appear on the masthead as one of three staff photographers. His role as one of the magazine's primary photographers continued intermittently until the magazine folded in 1967.[41] *Arts &*

Figure 23
*Maslon House,
photographed with
Richard Neutra, 1963,*
Cathedral City,
Richard Neutra, 1962

Figure 24
*Maslon House,
photographed without
Richard Neutra, 1963,*
Cathedral City,
Richard Neutra, 1962

23

24

Architecture was best known for its Case Study House Program, which was announced by Entenza in January 1945. The purpose of the program was to make well-designed single-family housing affordable for the typical post–World War II American family. The program spanned twenty-three years, from 1945 to 1967; thirty-six case study houses were proposed, twenty-six of which were actually constructed.[42] Of the houses that were built, Shulman photographed eighteen, presenting the dwellings with a visual consistency over the years.[43] His photographic compositions conveyed the houses boldly and effectively to the world, clearly documenting their place in the history of Southern California architecture. This is particularly evident in his classic 1960 view of Pierre Koenig's Case Study House #22 in the Hollywood Hills *(fig. 26)*. The photograph does not necessarily document the house but reflects an image of the postwar lifestyle that was to become representative of the modernity of California.[44]

Although Shulman did a great number of assignments for Entenza for more than twenty years, their relationship was strictly professional.[45] Shulman's professional relationship with Esther McCoy, on the other hand, developed into an important friendship. A large number of her essays in *Arts & Architecture* (and other magazines) were accompanied by Shulman photographs.

Shulman first met McCoy during their years of contributing to *Arts & Architecture*.[46] In 1948, when McCoy started to write for other magazines and newspapers, she asked them to commission photographs from Shulman.[47] In 1953 she "rediscovered" the George H. Wyman–designed Bradbury Building (which was then almost abandoned) in downtown Los Angeles. She immediately called Shulman to tell him of this "lost treasure that [he] must see and photograph." Shortly afterward, McCoy's essay, accompanied by Shulman's photographs, appeared in *Arts & Architecture,* restoring the building to the stature it deserved.[48] In 1956 the *Los Angeles Times* commissioned Shulman to photograph the Yucatan *(figs. 27, 28)* for McCoy's feature in its Home section. Shulman always speaks with the utmost respect for McCoy's ability to evoke architecture verbally.

From the late 1940s through the 1960s, Shulman made regular trips to New York to meet with magazine editors. Besides doing assignments for a large selection of architectural publications, in 1947 Shulman started working for popular and women's magazines, such as *Life* (1947–58), *House & Garden* (1946–64), *Ladies' Home Journal* (1948–62), and *Good Housekeeping* (1949–61).[49] In many ways he became the person who informed most of the editors on the East Coast of what was being built by established architects on the West Coast and lesser-known architects throughout the country. While East Coast photographers also worked in the West, Shulman's professional

Figures 25, 26
Case Study House #22,
1960, Los Angeles,
Pierre Koenig, 1959

25

27

28

Figure 27
The Pyramid of Castillo at
Chichén Itzá, 1956,
Yucatan, Mexico

Figure 28
The Pyramid of the
Magician at Uxmal, 1956,
Yucatan, Mexico

and personal circle of friends—mostly architects—placed him at the heart of the profession. His first job as a West Coast contributing photographer for *House & Garden* was the Frey House I *(fig. 29)*, located in Palm Springs and designed by Clark & Frey.[50] Shulman's masterful and systematic method of circulating his transparencies from one magazine to the next meant that this house was subsequently published internationally, with Clark and Frey hailed, in one publication, as "modern pioneers of the desert."[51] As Shulman's work for magazines grew in quantity, so did his listing of architectural clients. The magazine commissions also helped Shulman meet other architects outside of his Los Angeles circle, many of whom continued to hire him in order to insure a visual consistency and to place them in a league with established architects.[52] Furthermore, they doubtless knew that Shulman would promote their work at other magazines throughout the world; in this way Shulman became the photographer and de facto representative for many lesser-known architects.

House & Garden's architectural editor, Katherine Morrow Ford, thought so highly of Shulman's photographic "eye" that she hosted a cocktail party in his honor when he made his first trip to New York in 1947. The guests at this gathering included such major East Coast architects as William Lescaze, Edward Durrell Stone, and Walter Gropius, two of whom would become clients in the ensuing years. Shulman's working relationship with Ford hailed back to the late 1930s, when a large selection of his photographs was used in her book *The Modern Home in America*, published in 1940 and coauthored with her husband, James Ford.[53]

One of the few magazine editors who were impervious to the allure of Shulman's photographs was Elizabeth Gordon of *House Beautiful*. She chose not to use his work because, according to her, it depicted austere modern houses rooted in the European modern aesthetic, which she felt was too cold for the domestic dwellings of America.[54] In the pages of the April 1953 issue of *House Beautiful*, Gordon criticized modern architecture rooted in the International Style, viewing it as a possible political threat to the system of democracy: "If the mind of man can be manipulated in one great phase of life to be made willing to accept less, it would be possible to go on and get him to accept less in all phases of life." She believed that this type of architecture had social implications that could pose a "threat of cultural dictatorship" (in other words, Communism) to America. She further stated that the homes of this style reflected "poverty and unlivability." It was precisely this sort of criticism that put fear in American homeowners and fueled advertising strategies aimed at consumers, especially housewives.[55] During Gordon's time as editor of the magazine, austerely designed or furnished houses were rarely featured. After Gordon left *House Beautiful* in 1965, Shulman started to receive assignments from the magazine.[56]

29

Carl Norcross, associate editor of *House & Home* magazine, was one of the editors whom Shulman met with on a regular basis. In the mid-1950s, during one of his visits to New York, Shulman accepted an invitation from Norcross to dine at his home, only to realize upon arrival that Elizabeth Gordon was Norcross's wife. Shulman remembers, "It wasn't a pleasant evening." During dinner Gordon told Shulman that she thought his work was "cold." Shulman countered that many of the early buildings by Neutra, Soriano, and Davidson were pioneering in their design, but cold because of sparse furnishing, often due to the owners' depleted funds.[57] During the late forties and mid-fifties, magazines received letters condemning the publication of modern homes; even banks preferred not to grant loans for "modern, flat-roofed houses."[58] The general public did not understand modern architecture, and public opinion was paramount for Gordon. As the evening came to a close, Shulman conceded to Gordon that his photographs were not the kind that would attract *House Beautiful;* however, he was very busy with photographs for their competitor, *House & Garden.*[59]

Elizabeth Gordon's tendency to equate the authorship of a building with that of the photographer was problematic, for it was not Shulman's photographs that she disliked but their subject matter. In retrospect, she thought his photographs made the buildings look much better than they actually were.[60] Gordon disapproved of anything that might be rooted in European rhetoric and was a great supporter of Wrightian ideology. Numerous essays on Frank Lloyd Wright appeared in the magazine during her time as editor.[61] In contrast to Gordon, Wright thought very highly of Shulman's work. When Shulman was in Arizona to photograph the work of Blaine Drake (a Wright disciple) in 1950, Drake asked Shulman if he would be interested in meeting Wright at Taliesin. Drake made the arrangements and Shulman met Wright and stayed as his guest. While at Taliesin Shulman took photographs for himself, and when he returned to Los Angeles he sent a complete set of prints to Wright, thanking him for his hospitality.[62] In Wright's letter to Shulman it is obvious that he was taken with the photographs:

> When I let you in on Taliesin West I did not realize you were a professional photographer. I thought you were some artistic youth wanting to try your luck. Your work, however, is . . . better than a professional. Evidently you know what you are photographing.

> Meantime I suggest you take on the Morris Shop which I do not consider yet well done. . . . I admit that no better photos have been made of The Camp than those you sen[t]. What technique did you employ in making these admirable prints?[63]

Shulman's photographs of the V. C. Morris Gift Shop *(figs. 30–32),* taken in 1951, created a narrative of the building, making the plan of the shop clear to the viewer through a series of sequential views—from the exterior facade

Figure 29
Frey House I, 1947,
Palm Springs,
Clark & Frey, 1940

looking through the receding glass entrance to the interior ramp beyond. This photograph is countered by an interior view of the full ramp. However, the essential photograph in the series is an interior looking back through the telescopic entrance to a car at the curb. The ramp is implied in segments framing the lower right edge and the upper portion of the photograph.

From this time on, Shulman's commissions grew substantially throughout the United States as well as in Europe. He regularly scheduled visits for photo assignments and met with magazine editors. At one point he even thought of opening a small satellite office in New York. (When en route to New York to meet with editors, Shulman would often stop along the way for various photo assignments and have his negatives developed at a New York lab in time for his meeting.) However, he realized that splitting himself between both coasts would be chaotic and would affect his personal life.[64]

In the following decades Shulman became one of the most sought-after architectural photographers in the world. As more European publications commissioned Shulman for work in the United States, American publications were sending him to Europe on photo assignments.[65] In 1959 *Progressive Architecture* asked Shulman to do a photo essay on the modern architecture of Israel *(fig. 33)*. Though Shulman is a modernist at heart, his assignments included more than just buildings of the modern idiom: a *New York Times* commission, also of 1959, required him to photograph a traditional domestic dwelling in the Telemark countryside of Norway *(fig. 34)*.[66]

Figures 30–32
V. C. Morris Gift Shop,
1951, San Francisco,
Frank Lloyd Wright, 1948

Besides consistently creating quality photographs, Shulman also impressed many editors and professionals with his ability to deliver photographs on time and to produce a photographic narrative of the subject matter in which no two images were the same.[67] Shulman never bracketed his photographs; therefore, each composition on an assignment was different. In 1937 he stopped using a light meter and relied on his own judgment for the exposure. Shulman still asserts, "When I take a picture, I do it right the first time." The term *remainder* (photographs that do not turn out well) does not exist for him. In the mid-1960s, when the Modern Living editor of *Life* magazine asked to see his remainders of Herb Greene's "Prairie Chicken" House *(fig. 35)*, Shulman replied, "These are it; when I photograph a building I edit it photographically and architecturally. I am not going to waste my time or yours."[68] Furthermore, while on an assignment, it was not unusual for Shulman to take more than twenty photographs in one day. This sometimes allowed him to photograph more than one building per day.[69]

From 1950 onward, Shulman's photographic assignments expanded beyond architecture to ceramics and sculpture, as well as to commercial work for

30

31

32

33

34

35

manufacturers of building products. The photography for building products was conducted after he had completed assignments on large institutional or commercial buildings. Shulman would photograph areas such as the boiler room and then sell prints to the manufacturers whose products were used in the space. The manufacturers that purchased these photographs used them for marketing and advertisements in architectural and trade magazines. Many of these photographs treated the products as objects, with the same precise use of shade and shadow as in his photographs of buildings to enhance the forms of the machinery *(fig. 36).*[70]

The use of shade and shadow is also evident in Shulman's photography of ceramics and sculpture. In his photographs of Otto and Gertrud Natzlers' pottery *(figs. 37, 38)*, the surfaces of the objects are lighted to reveal a heightened texture and tactility. In 1964, Shulman was sent to England to photograph the works of Henry Moore for an article by Rosalind Wholden in *Arts & Architecture (figs. 39, 40)*. In the essay, Wholden speaks at length about Shulman's ability to reveal aspects of Moore's work rarely captured on film:

> Shulman's superb photo of the *Reclining Figure—Exterior Form,* by avoiding the usual parallel-to-the-picture-plane view of a horizontal sculpture, provides an experience of the tunneling, recoiling and shrouded feeling Moore has explored in countless serpentine excavations of the body. . . . The photographer . . . captures the surprising might of Moore's shapes; he encourages the timid onlooker to get close to the sculpture.[71]

Along with his professional career, Shulman has always been an educator. He has lectured on photography since the early 1940s.[72] Unlike many photographers who prefer to keep their methodology secret, Shulman enjoys sharing and discussing his craft with the public. Since 1958 he has written two books on the topic of photography and architecture as well as numerous essays. Shulman's essays range from conceptual to practical issues. His articles and books inform architects and designers of the important role that photography plays in creating the "memory image" of a building. He also explains more mundane issues like selecting a photographer and judging reasonable rates.[73]

Since the mid-1960s Shulman has conducted seminars on photography at numerous universities and institutions across the United States, such as the University of California at Los Angeles, the University of Southern California, Arizona State University, and Iowa State University, as well as divisions of the American Institute of Architects (AIA). Shulman's longest teaching stint, at Iowa State University's Continuing Education Department, lasted nine years. His seminars were usually held during the academic year and lasted four to five

Figure 33
Archeological Museum,
1959, Tel Aviv, Israel,
Wittkower & Baumann,
ca. 1955

Figure 34
Traditional Norwegian
House, 1959

Figure 35
Greene "Prairie Chicken"
House, 1961,
Norman, Oklahoma,
Herb Greene, 1961

36

39

37

38

40

days, depending upon the location of a particular building. Specific structures were used to illustrate points made in his books, teaching how to see "when the incision of light reveals the architecture." According to Shulman, anyone can learn how to use a camera, "but how to see, that is different."[74]

In 1984 Shulman conducted a workshop at the Ansel Adams Gallery in Yosemite *(fig. 41)*. Shulman originally met Adams in the fifties, and thirty years later, in early April 1984, they met again at Yosemite. After a long conversation Adams asked him to conduct a seminar on "The Architecture of Nature." Adams died at the end of that April; Shulman's seminar was held in September of the same year.[75]

It is appropriate that Shulman conducted a seminar at the Ansel Adams Gallery. Shulman's photographs (with and without buildings) have a quality that many feel resembles works by Adams. The similarity lies in their ideology; like many West Coast photographers of the 1930s, both adopted straight, finely focused photography. Both also understood the effects of over- and underexposure on the negative, which Adams later formalized in his "zone system."[76] In the mid-1930s, Shulman developed his own system of overexposing his film, reducing the shutter speed from $\frac{1}{100}$ of a second to $\frac{1}{50}$ of a second, and cutting the developing time in half. Shulman has used this process throughout his career, even with his later 4 x 5 and 8 x 10 format cameras.[77]

Shulman's significant contribution to architectural photography has been recognized since the 1960s, culminating in 1969 when he was awarded the highest honor the AIA can bestow on a photographer—the Architectural Photography Medal. The letters of support for Shulman's nomination are as demographically varied as his assignments. J. O. Hedrich of the Chicago-based architectural photography firm Hedrich-Blessing referred to Shulman as "Mr. Architectural Photography of the West Coast," while Jan C. Rowan, editor of *Progressive Architecture*, said, "His interest in the work of young architects all over the country has frequently provided us with interesting discoveries."[78] Yet one important name missing from these letters of support was that of Richard Neutra. The reason was purely logistical: from 1966 until June 1969 Dione and Richard were living in Vienna and traveling constantly.[79] Neutra was still in Vienna when he learned of the award and sent a letter to Shulman expressing his support. "I'd love to be decorating the table when you get that photography medal! Good, and the best to you. I wish an old architect could keep going as long as a photographer. But our dark rooms are darker than your darkrooms!"[80]

Shulman's professional career grew in many directions through both international commissions and awards honoring him for his outstanding contribution

Figure 36
Boiler Room, Los Angeles Department of Water and Power, 1965,
A. C. Martin and Associates, 1964

Figures 37, 38
Pottery, 1965,
Otto and Gertrud Natzler

Figure 39
Reclining Figure—Exterior Form, 1964,
Henry Moore, 1953–54

Figure 40
Two-Piece Knife Edge, 1964,
Henry Moore, 1962–63

41

to architectural photography. However, his personal life changed in September 1973 when Emma passed away while they were on vacation in Switzerland. Shortly after this loss Shulman's life changed again: he met Olga Heller through a mutual friend and in January 1976 they were married. Shulman always refers to himself as being very lucky in having married two of the world's greatest women.[81]

As a true modernist, Shulman naturally had a hard time accepting postmodern aesthetics as a viable architectural style. As postmodernism started to gain greater acceptance, Shulman refused to photograph this "type of bad architecture." During the mid-1970s, Shulman started to photograph historically important structures in the Los Angeles region. His archives reflect this diversity, from Victorian cottages to Wright buildings. Finally, in December 1986, Shulman decided to retire because he simply refused to photograph "bad buildings."[82] At this time postmodernism was at its height, and in Shulman's opinion, there were very few true practicing modernists left. His last official photo assignment (although he came out of retirement to rephotograph the Bradbury Building in 1991) was Pierre Koenig's recently completed house and studio in Brentwood *(fig. 43)*.[83]

Shulman's retirement was simultaneous, and in a way analogous, to the rediscovery, by both practicing architects and historians, of the modern movement. In 1987 his house and studio were landmarked by the Cultural Heritage Board of the City of Los Angeles as the only unmodified Soriano home designed of steel.[84] This reveals to some extent the fragility of the modern movement and how invaluable Shulman's photographs are in preserving this past. Although Shulman is retired, the constant demand for reprints from his vast collection has grown internationally.

In 1987 Shulman was made an honorary member of the AIA at its convention in Orlando, Florida, for his contribution to the profession. Ironically, another person honored that year was Elizabeth Gordon.[85] Neither had spoken to the other since their dinner in the mid-1950s, and during the course of the evening Shulman humorously asked Gordon—who did not respond—"How do you feel now about your views on Communism and European modern architecture?"[86]

Figure 41
Ahwahnee Hotel, 1984,
Yosemite

42

Method and Philosophy

As a strong believer in the notion of four sides of an artwork, Shulman is a formalist at heart, at times even testing his photographic compositions by flipping the stills to abstract the photograph and clarify the compositional frame *(fig. 42)*. Shulman's work is based on persuading the viewer to understand visually the architecture that he is depicting. This is a very important aspect of his success in making architecture accessible to the general public and was achieved through what he calls "diagonal thrust"[87]:

> I engage my viewers so their eyes follow the thrust of the lines that echo in my stills. The viewer is carried into the scene to where I want him to stop, look, and feel (sense) the architecture—not the photograph; it reads by subject matter and composition.[88]

There is an evolution in Shulman's photographic methodology from his pre-professional work in the early thirties through to his retirement in 1986. During these years, his inherent ability to "see" and compose luminous photographs has also been consistent. From his early pictures of Boulder Dam and Neutra and Schindler houses (taken with a vest-pocket camera) onward, Shulman demonstrates a timelessness and elegance in his compositions. By the late 1930s, Shulman used a 4 x 5 (and for a brief time an 8 x 10) format camera with various types of lenses that further enhanced his compositional ability by elongating the asymmetrically composed "synthetic" perspective of the photograph and thus achieving in these later works a greater sense of depth.[89] This sense of depth is further emphasized by his manipulation of light. The use of shade and shadow in a photograph delineates the subject matter, making it visible to the viewer. For Shulman,

> A shadow in a photograph is almost subliminal. . . . [It] echoes the structural elements of the design and reflects or mirrors the structure onto itself, creating a mood, . . . establishing an element of recall; that is, the embodiment of structure and form becomes established in the mind's eye.[90]

Shulman used shadows to mirror the characteristics of the buildings (and objects) he portrayed. His early ability to abstract from nature lends itself completely to his later abstractions of built form. For Shulman, there is order in nature; his early photographs are testimony of this. It is thus natural that his architectural photography would reflect the structure of the subject matter. His 1936 Boulder Dam photograph, taken with his vest-pocket camera, shows his innate sense of composition; the asymmetrical perspective is thrown into contrast by a series of geometric shadows that mirror the streamline forms of the

Figure 42
Santa Anita Racetrack
(printed upside down),
1938, Santa Anita

Figure 43
Koenig House and Studio,
1986, Los Angeles,
Pierre Koenig, 1985

bridge above *(fig. 44)*. Similar visual constructions are further enhanced in his later photographs, taken with a wide-angle lens. The photograph of Gregory Ain's Avenel Cooperative Apartments *(fig. 47)*, taken in 1949, illustrates the porte-cochere's patterned shadow, defining the receding frame of the perspective, which focuses on a small child riding a tricycle down the walkway toward the viewer.

In many ways Shulman has been an environmentalist since childhood. His knowledge of how light and shadow reveal order (and patterns) in nature stems from his early years on the farm in Connecticut as well as his later Boy Scout days in Los Angeles: "Being a Boy Scout, you must know how the sun works with nature—that knowledge is not site-specific, but fundamental."[91] Shulman would study a building in relationship to the landscape and the sun and, depending upon the orientation of the building, would structure his photographing sequence accordingly. His process embodies a sense of order that is evident in each of his photographs:

> When the front of a building is facing west and it's about 11:45 (at noon the sun will start to appear at the southwest corner of the building), I start to prepare for my photograph–camera position and compose the frame. At 12:00 the sun starts to appear at the south edge of my frame, bringing every detail of the west facade to life. . . . Light and shadow bring architecture to life at certain times of the day—you have to be ready to see it.[92]

In Shulman's photographs there is a marked difference between shade, which illustrates the form as well as the massing of a building, and shadow, which reveals texture. When he reviewed a building and its siting, he looked for elements that would be best portrayed in either shade or shadow. Shulman's use of shadow was not arbitrary: "The visual width of a shadow never exceeds the size of the object creating the shadow for the reason that it would misrepresent the true scale to the viewer." The shadow is used to dramatize, mirror, and at times contrast the object's inherent form and structure. The same principles were used for his interior photographs, which usually illustrate conditions of shade.[93]

In most of his photographs, Shulman used available light sources from the particular building to produce the lighting effects. If this was not possible, supplementary lighting was brought in.[94] The evolution of his lighting techniques is best illustrated by his descriptions of his 1947 efforts at Neutra's Kaufmann House in Palm Springs *(fig. 49)* and of his 1960 composition of Koenig's Case Study House #22 in Los Angeles *(fig. 26)*, with its vast difference in process (and available technology). Shulman recalls that for the 1947 photograph he had no assistance:

Figures 44–46
Boulder Dam, 1936, Boulder, Colorado

Figure 47
Avenel Cooperative Apartments, 1949, Los Angeles, *Gregory Ain, 1947*

44

It took me forty-five minutes to set up by myself, running back and forth between the house and the camera, turning on and off lights to balance the interior and exterior light value. All lighting for the photograph came from house light—no auxiliary lighting was used for the total exposure. The reclining figure next to the pool (Mrs. Kaufmann) was used to block the glare from the swimming pool light.[95]

The description of the photograph taken in 1960 is far more complex. By this time Shulman had had an assistant for almost a decade:

We always used our own lights to supplement the natural light in an interior, especially in an indoor-outdoor exposure of this kind. To balance the out-door light with the indoor light, I set up floodlights so that the glare of my lights would be absorbed behind the mullions and behind columns and fur-niture in the house. . . . After the floodlights were set, I had the girls sit down on chairs and told them that the lighting I set would be replaced with flashbulbs so that when I took the basic exposure there would be an instantaneous flash. . . . Next I told the girls to sit down in the dark with all the lights off, including the ceiling fixtures, and then began exposure for the lights in the distant . . . twilight that required a longer exposure. . . . I alerted the girls to sit up and get into conversational mood—they could continue to talk but be relaxed. We switched on the light on the ceiling and I flashed bulbs from my camera, and there was an instant flash regis-tering the furniture and the girls and the flash illuminated the ceiling out-side. Out of all that, this picture resulted.[96]

Figures 48, 49
Kaufmann House, 1947,
Palm Springs,
Richard Neutra, 1946

In fact, Shulman's "night shots" were never taken in true darkness, but at twilight, between seven and eight o'clock, when the sky "retained a glowing, form-revealing quality." In addition to this aesthetic explanation, his reasoning is based on logic. The envelope of a building cannot be defined if it is photo-graphed at night, and Shulman is very specific when he speaks of why this type of photograph must not be taken in darkness: "The overhang or edge of the building does not separate from the sky—there is no delineation, all that is illu-minated is the interior."[97] Shulman took his photographs when there was still enough definition on the ground plane, garden, and furniture (inside and out-side), as well as on the envelope of the house and the sky or mountains beyond.

The skies of Shulman's twilight photographs were actually "burned in" during the printing process to restore the lost tonal quality, thereby at times rendering the sky darker than it was when the photograph was taken.[98] For Shulman, "darkroom techniques are as much a part of the photographic process as clicking the camera shutter."[99] This has also allowed him to control the visual construction of each photograph, from the camera positioning to the dark-room process, as well as the time of day. These "night shots" create a sense of mood, an aura that was not actual but enhanced by Shulman's selective eye and darkroom process.

48

Shulman's photograph of the Kaufmann House had to have its sky tone restored in the darkroom. His writings reveal how and why he manipulated the photograph: "Photographing into the western sky shortly after sunset with prolonged exposure had destroyed the residual tones. They had to be restored in the darkroom. . . . Because of photographic limitations, a direct print from the original negative of this photograph was not desirable."[100] By manipulating the sky tone in the darkroom, Shulman was able to re-create a sunset with gradations of shadows over the mountains beyond, contrasting with the horizontality of the house in the foreground. This principle of restoration also applied to interior photographs: the careful manipulations of large horizontal surfaces, such as ceilings or floors, could infuse a tonal quality essential to the overall composition.[101]

Consequently, it is understandable that Shulman preferred black-and-white photography to color: "Black and white is more dramatic in its portrait, while color only adds a veneer to the picture."[102] He started shooting color as well as black and white in the early 1940s as more magazine editors requested color for their layouts.[103] This is still the case today; however, the use of color remains problematic for many photographers who use light and shadow in their work to create a certain aura. The photograph still reveals color tone, but it loses any sense of depth due to the lengthy exposure time of the film.[104] What makes black-and-white photography so timeless is the sense of contrast and depth dramatized by light and shadow. In some of Shulman's interior color photography he created conditions of light and shadow with added lighting; however, but inevitably "the strong contrast is in part lost due to the various tones of color in the frame."[105] Whenever Shulman took a color photograph he would also take a black and white of the same composition for the simple reason that the two mediums reveal different aspects of the subject matter: "Black and white . . . in its monochromatic state tends to emphasize form and tone at the expense of the total exposition possible by color photography."[106]

Shulman was one of few architectural photographers to use infrared film,[107] although he used it only when the weather or siting of the building created difficulties.[108] The inherent nature of the film brought out aspects that were not necessarily visible to the naked eye, thereby enhancing the photographic image, and when Shulman used infrared film in his later phase, the photographs became more embellished.[109] Most noteworthy is the brilliant depth of the sky plane juxtaposed against the building in the landscape. The use of infrared also created a greater sense of separation and depth in silhouetting the building against the landscape. Shulman's 1962 photograph of Frank Lloyd Wright's Sturges House in Los Angeles *(fig. 50)* could not have been otherwise accomplished. The main facade of the house was screened by a large eucalyptus tree. After setting up the composition and taking the photograph with regular film, Shulman realized the tonal value of the tree had blended together with the redwood of the house behind it. The use of infrared film rendered the green of the tree and shrubs white, so that they appear as featherlike elements outlining the house beyond, giving the photograph an added dimension of depth. It highlights what is there but not necessarily visible to the eye, and it also further shades the cloud formations, giving the sky a sense of greater depth and fullness.[110]

Some of Shulman's most memorable skies have been photographed when the weather was poor, as in the view of the United Covenant Presbyterian Church in Danville, Illinois, by Crites & McConnell *(fig. 51)*, taken in 1967. Shulman flew in for the assignment and upon arrival realized that the weather was just "too murky" to use his regular film, so he used infrared instead.[111] The photograph reveals intricate cloud formations, creating a sense of heightened drama in contrast to the geometrically austere lines of the church.

Shulman has been criticized for his use of infrared film because some people believe that it does not portray the true nature of a building. In response to this type of criticism he states: "I have always felt that this was a ridiculous attitude: the photographer can 'see' the potentials and, with [various types of] film, can go one step beyond dullness to produce something that is 'there,' but is not necessarily seen by the eye."[112] The issue of depicting a building in a "realistic" manner is problematic for the simple reason that the medium of photography is subjective and authorship of the photograph is separate from subject matter.[113] The photograph is not the building, but a representation of the image of the building, in other words, a duplication.

The notion of duplication is especially important in one aspect of Shulman's intuitive methodology. In addition to standard photographic duplication, Shulman reflects or mirrors—reduplicates—an image of the subject within the frame of the photograph.[114] This can be seen intermittently throughout Shulman's architectural photography, as well as in his 1935 Self-Portrait *(fig. 52)*. One of his earliest photographs, taken at Crystal Lake in 1930 *(fig. 54)*, shows his interest in using the mirror image (in this case, nature reflected in a lake) to represent the subject matter. In his 1933 *Portrait of Boats (fig. 53)*, the boats' hulls occupy the upper portion of the frame while their reduplication in the water occupies the rest of the frame and renders the photograph symmetrical about the horizontal axis. This sort of manipulation also occurs in his 1934 photograph of the Los Angeles City Hall, with the new Union Terminal Railroad Station under construction *(fig. 55)*. In the foreground, similar elements appear: the fractured repetition of the City Hall within pools of rainwater on

50

Figure 50
Sturges House, 1962
Los Angeles,
Frank Lloyd Wright, 1939

Figure 51
United Covenant
Presbyterian Church, 1967,
Danville, Illinois,
Crites & McConnell, 1967

Figure 52
Self-Portrait, 1935

the slab of the Union Terminal. Shulman continued to use this reduplication of subject matter in his professional photographs after 1936. Reduplication occurs horizontally (in pools of water, for instance) and also vertically (on glass walls). Horizontal mirroring literally duplicates the image of the building within the frame—in the reflective plane of the pool. Vertical duplication brings in subject matter (landscape or other buildings) from outside the frame. Shulman further enhanced this kind of duplication and reduplication of a building (or landscape) by using red filters, which emphasize the contrast between dark and light tones, and wide-angle lenses. Shulman's process of horizontal reduplication can be seen in many of his assignments that provided the proper conditions for the creation of this visual multiplicity; two particular examples are his 1947 photograph of Clark & Frey's Loewy House in Palm Springs *(fig. 56)* and his 1957 night shot of Neutra & Alexander's chapel at Miramar Naval Station in La Jolla *(fig. 57)*. The use of vertical reduplication is less frequent in Shulman's work and is best illustrated in his 1972 photograph of Langdon and Wilson's CNA Building in Los Angeles *(fig. 59)* and in his 1984 view of Johnson Burgee's Crystal Cathedral in Garden Grove *(fig. 58)*.

52

53

54

55

Figure 53
Portrait of Boats, 1933

Figure 54
Crystal Lake (printed upside
down), 1930

Figure 55
City Hall and Construction
of Union Terminal, 1934,
Los Angeles

Figure 56
Loewy House, 1947,
Palm Springs,
Clark & Frey, 1946

Figure 57
Miramar Naval Station
Chapel, 1957, La Jolla,
Neutra & Alexander, 1957

Figure 58
Crystal Cathedral, 1984,
Garden Grove,
Johnson Burgee, 1984

Figure 59
CNA Building, 1972,
Los Angeles,
Langdon and Wilson, 1972

58

83

60

61

Dressing the Photograph

Shulman relates photography to the production of cinema: "[The] camera's positions are not normally those from which a building or an interior is viewed. A good example of this can be demonstrated in a technique of motion-picture interior photography. A set often does not have walls; therefore, a scene of a living room is shot so that it has the effect of looking over the furniture arrangement at the action in the space."[115] The visual lines of the camera's lens inform and at times dictate the positioning of the furniture so that it reads correctly in the photograph. The perspective of the photograph is not necessarily true to the perspective of the actual space, but rather to the camera's view of it. Through the repositioning of furniture, Shulman's photographs become sets.[116] For example, when Shulman moved a couch from a wall to the center of the room and positioned the camera behind it, focusing on the center of the space, he illustrated a "space of action," placing the furniture in relation to an implied event. This can be further suggested by a table with place settings, objects displayed for a barbecue, or personal effects located throughout a space.

Shulman believes "the photographer is the director and producer of each frame," hence the author of each photograph.[117] It is commonly known that photographers, architects, and designers bring to an assignment props such as furniture, objects, and art. These objects provide the idealized image of the architecture. Shulman refers to this aspect of preparing a photograph as "dressing the scene." For instance, quite often when a building was completed and photographed for publication, the surrounding greenery was either not sufficiently grown in or the owner had depleted all funds in finishing the house. If these homes had been photographed against a barren landscape, the architecture would have looked unrelated to its context. To remedy the situation, Shulman would place branches on the earth in front of the building and position before the camera's cone of vision plants and tree branches from neighboring plots, thus creating a "frame" through which to photograph. Shulman maintains that one of the most important tools on a photo assignment is a pair of small garden clippers. On an assignment for *Good Housekeeping (figs. 60, 61),* he illustrated how he dressed the landscape with his "portable garden." Doing this allowed him to camouflage aspects not specific to the architectural character. Shulman would add greenery at different locations on the site, reconfiguring the plants so that they would not read as the same frame.[118] If an adjacent site had well-kept landscaping, Shulman would set up his camera from that site, positioning the camera at a lower level to photograph over the flowers in order to create the same effect.[119] The idea of enhancing exterior views of a building with props such as plants actually came from one of Shulman's earliest photo sessions with Neutra:

When I went to put my head under the focusing cloth [to look through the camera lens] I saw this windblown branch all of a sudden appear at the right edge of my frame, and at the bottom of it was Richard's hand. So I told him, "If you think we need to cover this area of the building, fine, but please let me fasten the branches to something because with your hands shaking it looks like a storm is coming."[120]

An implied frame could also be created with furnishings, as in his photograph of Koenig's Case Study House #22 *(fig. 26)*. Shulman remembers, "I had visualized the composition to the very edges of the overhang on the far right of the camera view, to the edge of the furniture composition inside, . . . and the chaise in the foreground framed the scene."[121]

The practice of dressing the photograph blurs the distinction between the "implied" and "actual" landscape, rendering it difficult at times to date the images of each building without documentation. In his commercially and promotionally commissioned architectural photography, the year of a building's completion is not always the same as the year of the photograph. This occurred for a variety of reasons. If the architect or the magazine wanted the photographs for publication shortly after the building was completed, Shulman would use his portable garden technique to decorate the landscape; if the building needed the mature vegetation of its own surroundings to illustrate the architectural intent, the photo shoot would be delayed accordingly.[122] Shulman rephotographed many of Neutra's buildings over the years because Neutra wanted photographs of his works in their mature settings and needed more illustrations of his previous architecture for his writings. Moreover, Neutra's works completed prior to his association with Shulman were rephotographed by Shulman; an example of this is Neutra's von Sternberg House of 1935 which was photographed by Shulman in 1947 *(figs. 62–64)*. The photographs depict the house with beautifully full-grown vegetation. When Shulman photographed the home it had already been sold by von Sternberg to the writer Ayn Rand, who appears with guests in the photographs.[123]

Figures 62–64
Von Sternberg House,
1947, Northridge,
Richard Neutra, 1935

62

63

64

Selling Architecture

Shulman believes that architectural photographers are in the business of "selling architecture" to the public.[124] This view stems from his strong conviction of the importance of good design and from the aesthetic code by which he lives. Before and immediately after World War II, modern architecture was welcomed by corporate America but rarely accepted by the public for domestic dwellings. Therefore, the photographs of these buildings had to come to life in the eyes of the viewer. In an interview, Shulman referred to the significant role and obligation of the photographer in creating the modern image: "He must realize that good design is seldom accepted. It has to be sold. So he's a propagandist, too. He must create subjective pictures, not snapshots. He must 'produce' moods through lighting. He must sell his subject."[125] The notion of "subjective pictures" is precisely what makes his photographs his own: they mirror a lifestyle intended to work within the framework of the design and its context. He knows that only when the project is understood by the photographer can "the finished pictures come alive in the eyes of the prospective purchaser of [a] product."[126] The photograph becomes the mediating tool between the subject and the viewer: it creates an "aura" for the viewer.[127] To achieve this, the photographer "must be able to dissect a structure or a design. He is a recorder—an historian, in effect, who is presenting the history of man, his housing, his activities."[128] Shulman is well aware of the dual role of the photographer as a seller of objects and as a visual recorder of history.

Furthermore, Shulman was an excellent businessman. He knew that popular consumer magazines and newspapers preferred to feature people in photographs, unlike the architectural magazines that only presented people when essential for scale.[129] Many of Shulman's commercial and domestic photographs include visual "witnesses" who illustrate how the spaces could be used. He is one of few architectural photographers of his generation to understand the importance of including individuals in the photograph[130]:

> I have always used people in my photographs. It is not just a matter of scale; it is a matter of bringing life to a scene. . . . [The Greenfield] house had his and hers workshops, all the accoutrements of 1950s living. In [one] photograph *[fig. 65]*, the woman is all dressed up making jewelry . . . in another photograph *[fig. 66]*, her husband is throwing a pot. The photographs were intended to show the "orderliness" of modern living, with the architecture as the key to a new lifestyle. People who live in a house can experience it, but the photographs show them, as well as others, how to "see" it.[131]

Figures 65, 66
Greenfield House, 1950,
Los Angeles,
Arthur Swab, ca. 1950

65

66

The placement of the witnesses in photographs of houses demonstrated exactly how they could be occupied. This made the homes seem more comfortable to the average American "consumer," paralleling trends in television and magazine advertising which illustrated people in "their homes."[132]

Shulman's photographs have multiple readings, for he injected a lifestyle (or work-style) into them. Most of his photographs have elements that imply activity within the frame. This was done to illustrate various aspects of the building—from details of the construction to the implied environment—that would appeal to the post–World War II consumer or corporation. In addition, most of the visual witnesses in these photographs actually occupied the office buildings or lived in the homes.[133]

Shulman's 1958 photographic construction of Buff, Straub and Hensman's Case Study House #20 *(fig. 67)* is conceptually and literally (by the column at the center of the frame) divided in two. A man occupies the left frame and a woman the right. Although positioned along the perimeter of the pool, the man is dressed in slacks and a shirt, while the woman wears a bathing suit, has a beverage, and sits at a higher elevation than the man. The positioning of the man and woman is specific to the building's relationship to nature. The woman is aligned with the pure, curved form of the fireplace. The man is aligned with the tree; his right arm actually mirrors the angle of the tree and extends to the position of his right leg. The fireplace (created) and the tree (natural) are the only elements that penetrate the horizontal roof plane of the house.

Shulman's photographs of Gordon Drake's home, taken in 1946, reveal another effect of dressing a photograph. One of the compositions *(fig. 70)* is constructed from the perspective of the viewer, who is presumably sitting on the couch or chair in the living room, looking toward other people seated on the terrace. By setting up the photograph in this manner, Shulman forces the viewer to participate in the scene: the viewer occupies the photograph, acting not as a voyeur but as a presence in the room. This lower vantage point also reveals aspects of the home that would otherwise not be visible: the ceiling details and the landscape beyond the terrace.[134]

The vantage point in the 1959 photograph of the Skinner House *(fig. 71)* is that of a stuffed toy animal. This rendered the children taller than usual, so that their scale reads as adult. The boys/men are on the terrace playing with army toys; the girl/woman is inside the house playing with her doll carriage in front of the sliding glass doors. The photograph illustrates the typical domestic and gendered roles of children (and adults). However, photographs do not necessarily need witnesses in order to render a

Figure 67
Case Study House #20
(Bass House), 1958,
Altadena,
Buff, Straub and Hensman,
1958

69

70

Figures 68–70
Drake House, 1946,
Los Angeles,
Gordon Drake, ca. 1945

71

72

space occupiable. Shulman's 1951 photograph of Neutra's Kester Avenue Elementary School *(fig. 72)* records the space prior to the students' arrival for class; parallel to the camera is a list of things little children should know. To illustrate Neutra's idea of a classroom opening to the outside, even to outdoor classes, the composition of the play furniture forms a semi-circle that extends from inside the classroom through open glass doors to the exterior.

Shulman's photographs illustrate occupied spaces whether a person actually appears in the frame or if there is simply an implied presence. This renders the space occupiable by the viewer of the photograph.[135] When people are placed within the frame, they become signs of events taking place and are depicted in the lifestyle or manner appropriate to the home or building. At times Shulman's photographs relegate the architecture to the status of backdrop to events. Many architects approved of this, believing it put houses in context and emphasized the functions of the home.[136] If Shulman had not employed these methods, many of the buildings would read as sterile, unoccupiable spaces. Shulman himself has said that some of the buildings he photographed "appeared cold and literally lifeless and needed people [in them] to come alive."[137] This was an alluring way to lead the viewer's gaze into the architecture and the ideal life that went with it.

Figure 71
Skinner House, 1959,
Los Angeles,
Robert Skinner, ca. 1955

Figure 72
Kester Avenue Elementary
School, 1951,
Los Angeles,
Richard Neutra, 1951

The Historical Frame

Architecture has provided primary subject matter throughout the history of photography.[138] Since the mid-1920s numerous art photographers have been commissioned at one time or another to do professional architectural photography for popular consumer and architectural magazines. Margaret Bourke-White, for instance, started out as an architectural photographer with assignments for architectural firms; her first published photographs appeared in the February, April, and July 1928 issues of *House & Garden*, followed by *Architectural Forum* in 1931.[139] The practice of embellishing a building's surroundings is also evident in her early architectural photographs.[140] Well known for his distortion photographs, André Kertész was a staff photographer for *House & Garden* from 1945 to 1962, documenting many dwellings on the East Coast.[141] The classic 1930 photographs of Mart Stam's architecture in Frankfurt, Germany *(fig. 75)*, were taken by the art photographer Ilse Bing at the beginning of her career.[142] And Cologne photographer August Sander also received commissioned architectural assignments *(fig. 76)*, although he is best known for his portraiture.[143] One of few architectural photographers to receive an elevated status internationally among collectors and historians was the German photographer Werner Mantz *(fig. 78)*.[144] Each of these photographers has helped to dissolve the boundaries of architectural photography, including artistic compositions along with straightforward documentary images, and bringing recognition to other talented practitioners in the field.[145]

One plausible reason for architectural photography's delayed acceptance may be that in the early twentieth century, "the countries that developed the new modern architecture, the Netherlands, Germany, and France . . . did not develop a new style for photographing it," with the exception of works by Lucia Moholy *(fig. 77)* and Werner Mantz.[146] By contrast, the countries that embraced modern architecture as an import, such as Britain and the United States, did develop a new style to present the architecture to a general public.[147] Furthermore, the architectural photography of the United States was more progressive than that of Britain. In 1937 the magazines *Architectural Record* in New York and *Architectural Review* in London traded editorial services for their March issues. In Robert Elwall's essay "The Specialist Eye," he compared the constructed images of the photographs that were illustrated in these two issues and concluded:

> [The London based] Dell and Wainwright *[fig. 79]* were more conservative in their interpretation of modern architecture than American photographers such as F. S. Lincoln *[fig. 80]*, his country's leading pre-War professional. After the War Lincoln's mantle was assumed by [Ken Hedrich of] Hedrich-Blessing in Chicago *[fig. 74]*, . . . Ezra Stoller in New York *[fig. 73]*, . . . and the Los Angeles–based Julius Shulman. [Their photographs of modern architecture] greatly influenced architects in Britain and elsewhere and helped consolidate the Modern Movement.[148]

Figure 73
Chamberlain Cottage, photographed by Ezra Stoller, 1942,
Wayland, Massachusetts, Marcel Breuer and Walter Gropius, 1940

Figure 74
Fallingwater, photographed by Ken Hedrich (Hedrich-Blessing), 1937,
Mill Run, Pennsylvania, Frank Lloyd Wright, 1935

73

74

Figure 75
Staircase, photographed
by Ilse Bing, 1930,
Frankfurt, Germany,
Mart Stam

Figure 76
Dr. Lehmann Apartment,
photographed by August
Sander, ca. 1929,
Dresden, Germany

75

76

77

78

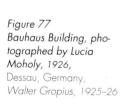

Figure 77
Bauhaus Building, photographed by Lucia Moholy, 1926,
Dessau, Germany,
Walter Gropius, 1925–26

Figure 78
Apartment House, photographed by Werner Mantz, 1928,
Cologne, Germany

99

Figure 79
*Car Service Station,
photographed by Dell
and Wainwright, 1934,*
Staines, Middlesex, England,
Cameron Kirby, 1934

Figure 80
*"Five by Five" Phelps-
Dodge integrated bathroom,
photographed by F. S.
Lincoln, 1936,*
Buckminster Fuller, 1936

The major difference between modern architecture in Britain and the United States is that when the aesthetic arrived in America, it lost its political character and became a metaphor for a better life. When *New York Times* architecture critic Paul Goldberger reviewed the Museum of Contemporary Art retrospective on the California Case Study House Program, he opened his article with a discussion on the promise of progress implied in Shulman's famous photograph of Koenig's Case Study House #22 *(fig. 26)*:

> In 1960 the architectural photographer Julius Shulman took a picture of a glass house perched high in the Hollywood Hills that will always be, for me, one of those singular images that sum up an entire city at a moment in time. The house is sleek and white, and its glass walls are cantilevered out over the hills; two elegantly dressed women lounge inside as the lights of the vast sprawl of the Los Angeles basin twinkle below. Here was the modern world, fresher and newer than in the East; [it] possessed a visual drama that the cities of the East Coast could only dream of and yet with all of their luxury and style.[149]

In many respects, Shulman's photographs reflect the aesthetic characteristics of the decades during which he worked. His type of architectural photography had a "propagandizing style . . . that created seductive statements."[150] Variations on this style can be seen in the works of other architectural photographers in the United States: East Coast–based F. S. Lincoln, Ezra Stoller, and R. Damora; Chicago-based Ken Hedrich; and West Coast–based Roger Sturtevant, Maynard L. Parker, Fred R. Dapprich, Marvin Rand, and Morly Baer; and in Britain in the works of Dell and Wainwright, Herbert Felton, and John Havinden. Some of the successful photographers adopted this style because they needed to sell modern architecture through the magazines as a product of technology, progress, and consumption.[151]

Shulman's photographs of California, like Eugène Atget's views of Paris, have become memory images for us. They embody the modernity, myths, and realities of the landscape as well as a lifestyle that has become equated in the minds of Americans and Europeans alike with the essence of the West Coast. Since the modern movement has itself become a historical subject, the people who gave us these images play an essential role in the creation of that history. The physical building is rarely experienced, so its timeless character must be embodied in the photograph. The photograph therefore becomes the lens through which a discourse can be formulated to analyze, critique, and reassess the evolution of architecture and its representation. Historically, the role of the architectural photographer has been that of a chronicler of visual conditions of structures and, simultaneously, a creator of visual "signs" of culture. Shulman's photographs embody the spirit and memory of the past pioneers of modernism, transporting the viewer back to a time when buildings, landscape, and people were in harmony with one another.

ENDNOTES

All interviews were conducted by the author. The several interviews with Julius Shulman are identified by "Shulman" and the date of the interview.

1.   Shulman, June 18, 1991, and January 20, 1993.

2.   Shulman, June 18, 1991, and January 20, 1993.

3.   Shulman, June 18, 1991, and January 20, 1993; Judy McKee (Shulman's daughter), interview, January 21, 1993.

4.   Shulman, June 22, 1991.

5.   Shulman, June 18, 1991.

6.   Shulman, June 18, 1991, and January 20, 1993.

7.   Shulman, June 18, 1991, and January 20, 1993. See also Chris Flacke and Kathy Lindstrom, "Comments on Buildings: An Interview with Julius Shulman," *Offramp*, Fall 1990, 6.

8.   Shulman, June 18, 1991. Shulman remembers this, but there is no documentation in his archives or in the Bourke-White archives. The Margaret Bourke-White Papers, Department of Special Collections, Syracuse University Library; Shulman, June 22, 1991; photographic caption, Esther McCoy, "Persistence of Vision: The Encompassing Eye of Architectural Photographer Julius Shulman," *Angeles*, March 1990, 91.

9.   Shulman, June 18, 1991.

10.   Shulman, June 18, 1991.

11.   The name of this friend is unknown because Shulman lost touch with him shortly after this time, but Shulman does recall that this man had worked for Walter Dorwin Teague on the East Coast before working for Neutra. However, the documents at the Neutra Collection are very sparse prior to 1940 and do not contain a list of employees for this period, and the job file for the 1935 Kun House does not cite specific individuals who worked on the building. The office of Walter Dorwin Teague Associates retains employee records dating back to the early 1930s, but this man could not be identified. Shulman, June 18, 1991; Aileen Gaugahn, Walter Dorwin Teague Associates, interview, March 8, 1993; the Richard J. Neutra Collection, Department of Special Collections, library of the University of California, Los Angeles.

12.   Thomas S. Hines, "Julius Shulman in 40th Year," *L.A. Architect*, December 1976, 1; Shulman, June 18, 1991; McKee, interview, January 21, 1993.

13.   Thomas S. Hines, *Richard Neutra and the Search for Modern Architecture* (New York: Oxford University Press, 1982), 140–41; Shulman, June 22, 1991.

14.   Shulman, June 18, 1991; Shulman's logbook of photographic assignments, Shulman Archives, Shulman Holder.

15.   Shulman, June 22, 1991.

16.   Shulman, June 18, 1991.

17.   Shulman, June 18, 1991; Shulman logbook, Shulman Archives.

18.   While Shulman was in the army, requests for reproductions from his slide and photographic collections were fulfilled by his wife, Emma, who worked from her mother's house. The reproductions were made in a photo lab. Shulman, letter to the author, February 1, 1993.

19.   Shulman, October 24, 1992; McKee, interview, January 21, 1993.

20.   Shulman's black-and-white printing was done by Julius Frank starting in 1949. Born near Bremen, Frank (1900–1959) was schooled in photography in Germany and was himself an accomplished photographer. His family had been involved in photography since its inception. At a relatively early age Frank became a master photographer with his own apprentices and studio and was also proprietor of a camera shop. In 1936 Frank and his wife, Hildegard, left Germany for America, and by 1947 they had settled in Los Angeles. Julius Frank did all of Shulman's black-and-white processing and at times assisted Shulman on assignments. Hildegard also worked intermittently, producing prints for a commercial photo lab, as well as working with her husband to produce large quantities of reprints. In 1959, when Julius Frank died of a heart attack in Mexico, Hildegard assumed his role in the studio, producing all of Shulman's black-and-white prints until 1986, when he retired. From then on, Shulman worked closely with a local film lab under established guidelines for the printing of his photographs. Color processing was never done in the studio, but was sent out to a color lab, again under Shulman's close supervision. From 1961 through 1986, Carlos Von Frankenberg worked as Shulman's assistant on assignments. Shulman, October 24, 1992; Hildegard Frank Ober, interview, April 17, 1993; McKee, interview, January 21, 1993; Shulman Archives.

21.   Shulman, March 15, 1991. According to the Shulman Archives and the Neutra Collection, Shulman photographed over 250 of Neutra's 300 buildings.

22.   A brief overlap occurs between Shulman and Luckhaus Studios from 1936 through 1937. Luckhaus photographed Neutra's works from 1929 through 1937 (building dates), and from the appearance of the vegetation in these photographs, it is likely they were taken shortly after the buildings' completions. None of the photographs by Luckhaus Studios in the Neutra Collection are precisely dated. Moreover, there is no documentation to explain why Neutra no longer commissioned Luckhaus after 1937.

Willard D. Morgan (1900–68) photographed for Neutra from around 1927 until April 1930. In August 1930 he moved to New York. Morgan also photographed buildings and interiors by J. R. Davidson, Kem Weber (until 1930), and Frank Lloyd Wright and Louis Sullivan (1930–32). Lloyd Morgan, interview, January 27, 1993; Willard & Barbara Morgan Archives, Morgan & Morgan Press, Dobbs Ferry, New York.

23.   The exception to this is the photographs taken by Luckhaus and Morgan of Neutra's Lovell House of 1927–29. However, this is mostly due to the siting of the house, which necessitates including the context in any exterior photograph of the building.

24.   Neutra was well aware of this aspect in the formation of his international career. In a letter to Vreneli and Ruben, dated November 29, 1929, he states:

> I am sending you a few photographs of the Lovell Demonstration Health House. As yet it has not been published anywhere. . . . Could you possibly send it with the enclosed English text to a Scandinavian or Argentinian illustrated weekly magazine? I would indeed be most grateful.

> California, Hollywood-American-modern, architecture finds a certain interest everywhere.

Dione Neutra, ed., *Richard Neutra, Promise and Fulfillment 1919–1932: Selections from Letters and Diaries of Richard and Dione Neutra* (Carbondale and Edwardsville: Southern Illinois University Press, 1986), 180. For more on this aspect of Neutra's career, see Hines's definitive *Richard Neutra and the Search for Modern Architecture*.

25.   For more on the photographs used for this exhibition, see Terence Riley's thoroughly documented book *International Style: Exhibition 15 and The Museum of Modern Art* (New York: Rizzoli and Columbia Books of Architecture, 1992), 79–80, 209nn. 25, 26. In Philip Johnson's letter to Richard Neutra (October 26, 1931), he wrote that the exterior view he had submitted of the Lovell "Health" House looked too barren. Neutra's response to Johnson (October 30, 1931) said that new photographs would be taken for the exhibition. The photographs Neutra originally submitted for both constructed buildings in the exhibition were taken by Willard D. Morgan. The Jardinette Apartments were photographed in 1927, and the Lovell "Health" House was photographed intermittently from December 12, 1929, to April 23, 1930. The photographs of the Lovell House with mature vegetation were taken by Luckhaus Studios, most likely between the end of 1931 and early 1932. (The exhibition opened in February 1932.) At the exhibition, the interior photograph of the house was by Morgan (from 1930) and the exterior by Luckhaus. Johnson's letter and Neutra's response are in the Registrar's Archive, The Museum of Modern Art, New York. Also consulted were the Morgan Archives and the Neutra Collection.

26.   Dione Neutra, letter to Shulman, April 18, 1969, Shulman Archives.

27.   Chloetheiel Woodward Smith, "In a House Neutra Built," *Washington Post*, July 1, 1956.

28.   Richard J. Neutra, letter, January 29, 1969, Shulman Archives.

29.   Shulman, September 25, 1992.

30.   Richard J. Neutra, letter, January 29, 1969, Shulman Archives.

31.   Shulman, September 25, 1992. Also, Flacke and Lindstrom, "Comments on Buildings," 6.

32.   Shulman, September 25, 1992. Also, Flacke and Lindstrom, "Comments on Buildings," 6.

33.   Esther McCoy, "The Important House," *The New Yorker*, April 1948, excerpted in *Architecture California*, May 1992, 35, with statement by Julius Shulman. Also, Shulman, October 31, 1992.

34.   Shulman, September 25, 1992. Also, Flacke and Lindstrom, "Comments on Buildings," 8.

35.   Shulman, June 22, 1991.

36.   Shulman, June 22, 1991; Raphael Soriano, interview, November 11, 1987. Also, Esther McCoy, *The Second Generation* (Salt Lake City: Peregrine Smith Books, 1984), 161.

37.   Shulman, June 22, 1991. It should be noted that Neutra considered Soriano his disciple and that Soriano received fewer commissions in comparison. However, if Shulman had commissioned Schindler, matters might have been more complicated, because at this point Neutra and Schindler were not on speaking terms. For more on the relationship between Neutra and Schindler see David Gebhard, *Schindler* (Salt Lake City: Peregrine Smith, 1980); Thomas S. Hines, *Richard Neutra and the Search;* and Stefanos Polyzoides, "Schindler, Lovell and the Newport Beach, Los Angeles, 1921–1926," *Oppositions* 18 (1979).

38.   Philip Johnson, interview, May 28, 1987; Thomas S. Hines, interview, August 25, 1992; David Gebhard, interview, August 24, 1992.

39.   Shulman, September 25, 1992.

40.   Shulman, September 25, 1992. For a log of Shulman's commissioned assignments for publications, see the client list.

41.   Shulman, March 15, 1991. Shulman's name appeared on the masthead of the magazine until 1958, when the masthead no longer listed staff photographers.

42.   Esther McCoy, *Case Study Houses 1945–1962* (Los Angeles: Hennessey & Ingalls, 1977); Elizabeth A. T. Smith, ed., *Blueprints For Modern Living: History and Legacy of the Case Study Houses* (exhibition catalog, Cambridge: MIT Press, 1989).

43.   Contact prints and film negatives of each case study house are identified in the Shulman Archives by their built number (see below) and year, and listed under the heading of *Arts & Architecture* magazine; any subsequent photographs taken are listed under the heading of the architect. The eighteen buildings that Shulman photographed are: Case Study House #1 (actually number #11) by J. R. Davidson, 1946; #3 by Wurster and Bernardi, 1949; #8 by Ray and Charles Eames, 1949; #9 by Charles Eames and Saarinen, 1949; #10 by Nomland and Nomland, 1947; #15 by J. R. Davidson, 1947; #16 by Rodney A. Walker, 1947; #17 by Rodney A. Walker, 1947; #20 by Richard Neutra, 1948; #20 by Buff, Straub and Hensman, 1958; #21 by Pierre Koenig, 1958; #22 by Pierre Koenig, 1959; #23 Triad (all three houses photographed by Shulman) by Killingsworth, Brady and Smith, 1960; #25 by Killingsworth, Brady and Smith, 1963; #28 by Buff, Hensman & Associates, 1966; and Soriano's unnumbered Case Study House of 1950.

McCoy's book *Case Study Houses 1945–1962* explains why some numbers for these houses appear twice:

> In several instances the same number was assigned twice: #16, #17, and #18 by Rodney A. Walker, completed in 1947 and 1948, were reassigned to Craig Ellwood, whose Case Study Houses #16, #17, and #18 were completed in 1952, 1955, and 1957.
>
> Richard Neutra's CSH #20, completed in 1948, reappeared in the 1958 CSH #20 by Buff, Straub and Hensman. CSH #21, a 1947 unexecuted Neutra project, turned up again as Pierre Koenig's CSH #21, completed in 1958.
>
> J. R. Davidson's CSH #1 and #11 were transposed when #1 was abandoned and #11 was the first CSH to be completed, furnished, landscaped and opened to the public (210).

44.   The photographic depiction of these buildings is extremely important, but essays in the exhibition catalog *Blueprints For Modern Living* make no mention of the visual records that Shulman or other photographers (including Ernest Braun, Jason Hailey, Marvin Rand, and James Reed) constructed. Because of the visual continuity of the photographs, Entenza's program was compared to that of *siedlungs* in Europe. In fact, these houses have a stronger connection with the individual "model homes" featured in American women's magazines and architectural journals. In addition, this misreading might be attributed to the publication of Esther McCoy's *Modern California Houses* (published in 1962 and reprinted in 1977 as *Case Study Houses 1945–1962*) which collectively illustrated all twenty-six houses in one volume. McCoy's book was not a facsimile of the previously published pages from *Arts & Architecture.* In the magazine each photograph was accompanied by a lengthy caption listing each piece of furniture and its manufacturer. Hence, each case study house that was showcased in the magazine became an advertisement for the manufacturer. In McCoy's book these captions are not used; instead, captions address issues of spatiality and construction technique. Therefore, the way in which these houses were published in the magazines was very different from the way they were presented in McCoy's book. For more on this issue see Reyner Banham, "Architecture IV: The Style That Nearly . . ." in *Los Angeles: The Architecture of Four Ecologies* (New York: Harper & Row, 1971), 223–34. Also see David Gebhard's review of *Blueprints For Modern Living,* in *Journal of the Society of Architectural Historians* 50, no. 2 (June 1991): 221–22.

45.   Shulman, March 15, 1991.

46.   Shulman, June 22, 1991.

47.   Shulman's card catalog of clients contains entries under Esther McCoy Tobey. These assignments were paid for by the publisher that commissioned the articles from McCoy. The entries span eleven years, from 1948 to 1959, and total forty-five photo assignments. This figure, however, does not reflect McCoy's numerous other essays that were illustrated with Shulman's stock photographs of works by Neutra, Schindler, Soriano, and others. Shulman Archives; Barbara J. Dawson, letter to the author, November 24, 1992; the Esther McCoy Papers, Archives of American Art, Smithsonian Institution, Washington, D.C.

48.   Shulman, June 22, 1991. Also, Esther McCoy, "The Bradbury Building," *Arts & Architecture,* April 1953, 20–21. According to the client file cards in the Shulman Archives, Shulman has photographed the Bradbury Building a total of five times: in 1953, 1967, 1969, 1970, and 1991.

49.   Shulman, October 31, 1991; Shulman Archives.

50.   Shulman, October 31, 1991; Albert Frey, interview, July 10, 1992; Shulman Archives.

51.   "Un Ospedale a Palm Springs," *Domus,* July-August 1952, 12–13.

52.   Frey, interview, July 10, 1992; Gebhard, interview, August 24, 1992; Hines, interview, August 25, 1992; Edward Killingsworth, interview, August 25, 1992; Pierre Koenig, interview, September 5, 1992.

53.   Shulman, October 31, 1991. Katherine Morrow Ford was an architectural editor at *House & Garden* from September 1945 to July 1949 and a consulting architectural editor from July 1949 to October 1951.

54.   Elizabeth Gordon, interview, August 25, 1992.

55.   Elizabeth Gordon, "The Threats to the Next America," *House Beautiful,* April 1953, 127. Gordon's article states the position of the magazine under her direction:

> *House Beautiful* finally speaks up to point plainly to the nonsense that goes on in the name of "good design." For, if you are aware of what is happening, we believe you will be quite competent to handle the matter for yourself. We still operate on common sense and reason. We know that less is not more. It is simply less!

In that issue another article, "Cubism and the International Style," plays on the same theme of simplification and generalization, in order to further warn American women against the "European" influence. However, it also makes some very insightful statements regarding the institutionalization of the International Style in America via academia: "International Stylists are still playing with blocks 30-odd years after Picasso went on to something else. Posing as the avant-garde, they are in reality the Beaux Arts of the Twentieth Century, the new academicians of an old-fashion esthetic" (240). The magazine, under the direction of Gordon, went to great lengths to make its views known to its audience with articles citing homes of this aesthetic as being a "good example of bad architecture." In Joseph Barry's article "Good and Bad Modern Houses" (May 1953), he cites Mies's Farnsworth House as "a particularly fine example of a bad modern house." Having interviewed the "dissatisfied owner," he goes on to quote Dr. Edith Farnsworth at great length (270). Barry also refers directly to the role of photographers: "They usually fail to look into what these architects have actually built. . . . At most they see deceptive photographs, pictures taken from a flattering angle that lend a false glamour" (272).

56.   Shulman, March 15, 1991, and June 22, 1991. Shulman's first assignment for *House Beautiful* was in 1968. Shulman client file cards, Shulman Archives. Also, Gordon file, American Institute of Architects (AIA) Library and Archives, Washington, D.C.

57.   Shulman, March 15, 1991, and June 22, 1991.

58.   Elaine Sewell Jones, interview, March 15, 1991; Frey, interview, July 10, 1992.

59.   Shulman, June 22, 1991.

60.   Gordon, interview, August 25, 1992.

61.   Three major issues were published on the work of Frank Lloyd Wright: November 1955, October 1959, and a 1963 issue devoted to the Hanna House.

62.   Shulman, January 20, 1993.

63.   Frank Lloyd Wright, letter to Shulman, August 9, 1950. Shulman Archives.

64.   Shulman, June 18, 1991.

65.   Shulman, June 18, 1991. Also, Shulman's logbook shows an increase in international assignments, as do his client file cards. Shulman Archives.

66.   Shulman, June 18, 1991.

67.   Shulman, October 24, 1992; Killingsworth, interview, August 25, 1992; Frey, interview, July 10, 1992; Koenig, interview, September 5, 1992.

68.   Shulman, June 18, 1991, and June 22, 1991.

69.   Shulman logbook and client file cards, Shulman Archives.

70.   Shulman, October 24, 1991.

71.   Rosalind Wholden, "Henry Moore: Deukalion of Modern Sculptors," *Arts & Architecture*, January 1965, 22–24, 33.

72.   Shulman papers, Shulman Archives.

73.   Shulman, June 18, 1991. Also, see the selected bibliography.

74.   Shulman, June 18, 1991. Also, Shulman papers, Shulman Archives.

75.   Shulman, June 18, 1991. Also, Shulman papers, Shulman Archives.

76.   Ansel Adams, *Ansel Adams: Images 1923–74* (Boston: New York Graphic Society, 1974).

77.   Shulman, June 18, 1991.

78.   Shulman, October 24, 1991. Also, Shulman file, Architectural Photography Medal, AIA Library and Archives.

79.   Hines, *Richard Neutra and the Search*, 295.

80.   Neutra, letter to Shulman, March 18, 1969. Shulman Archives.

81.   Shulman, June 22, 1991; McKee, interview, January 21, 1993.

82.   Shulman, June 18, 1991.

83.   Shulman, June 22, 1991.

84.   In November 1983 Esther McCoy made the official request that Shulman's house become a historic-cultural monument. The application describes the architectural features as "wholly out of 20th-century technology: all elements, from steel bents of the frame to the storage cabinet room dividers, were factory-produced and hauled to the site in trucks." The document concludes: "The steel-framed house is known throughout Europe and Japan as a Southern California phenomenon, and Soriano was the first to exploit the system fully. The romantic Shulman house is the only Soriano in the city still in its original state." The declaration was approved by three members of the Cultural Heritage Board on June 3, 1987. The Cultural Heritage Board, Cultural Affairs Department, Los Angeles.

85.   Shulman, October 24, 1991. Also, Tony Wrenn, AIA Archivist and Hon. AIA/California Archivist, interview, December 2, 1992. Seven people became honorary members of the AIA in 1987. The Shulman files for honorary membership is incomplete; his letters and list of sponsors are missing. The file on Elizabeth Gordon's nomination is complete and the people who supported her nomination reveal the strong support and respect she had from Wrightian followers. Her sponsors included Harwell Hamilton Harris, John Lautner, Charles Montooth (Taliesin Associated Architects), Edgar Tafel, and Bruno Zevi. AIA Library and Archives.

86.   Shulman, October 24, 1991.

87.   Shulman, October 24, 1991. Shulman also refers to this as "dynamic symmetry." He credits his cousin, who taught art in Detroit, for discovering this consistency in his early photographs.

88.   Shulman, June 22, 1991.

89.   "A perspective that tends to flatten, to fragment, to generate ambiguous overlap, to which Galassi gives the name 'analytic,' as opposed to the 'synthetic' constructive perspective of the Renaissance, was fully developed by the late eighteenth century within the discipline of painting." For more on analytic and synthetic perspectives, see Rosalind E. Krauss, "Photography's Discursive Space," in *The Originality of the Avant-Garde and Other Modern Myths* (Cambridge: MIT Press, 1986), 135. Krauss's text is in part a response to Peter Galassi's exhibition catalog *Before Photography: Painting and the Invention of Photography* (New York: Museum of Modern Art, 1981).

90.   Julius Shulman, *The Photography of Architecture and Design* (New York: Whitney Library of Design, 1977), 51.

91.   Shulman, June 22, 1991.

92.   Shulman, June 22, 1991.

93.   Julius Shulman, *Photographing Architecture and Interiors* (New York: Whitney Library of Design, 1962), 62–63. Also, Shulman, June 22, 1991.

94.   Shulman, June 18, 1991.

95. Shulman, June 18, 1991.

96. Flacke and Lindstrom, "Comments on Buildings," 8.

97. Shulman, June 22, 1991, and September 25, 1992. Also, Shulman, *Photographing Architecture and Interiors*, 71.

98. Shulman, *Photographing Architecture and Interiors*, 81.

99. Shulman, *Photographing Architecture and Interiors*, 84.

100. Shulman, *The Photography of Architecture and Design*, 71. Also, Shulman, *Photographing Architecture and Interiors*, 70.

101. Shulman, *The Photography of Architecture and Design*, 71. Also, Shulman, *Photographing Architecture and Interiors*, 70.

102. Shulman, June 22, 1991.

103. Shulman, June 22, 1991.

104. Thomas Fisher, "Image Building," *Progressive Architecture*, August 1990, 89.

105. Shulman, June 22, 1991.

106. Julius Shulman, "An Emphasis on Shape," *Applied Photography* 45 (Rochester, N.Y.: Eastman Kodak, 1970), 13.

107. Shulman, June 22, 1991. Also, Cervin Robinson, interview, January 22, 1993; Norman McGrath, interview, January 22, 1993; Marvin Rand, interview, August 24, 1992; Ezra Stoller, interview, August 14, 1992.

108. Shulman, letter to the author, August 21, 1992.

109. Shulman, June 22, 1991. According to Tod Justavson, assistant curator of the Technology Collection, George Eastman House, Rochester, New York, infrared film was not intended for still commercial photography but for scientific use.

110. Shulman, June 22, 1991.

111. Shulman, *The Photography of Architecture and Design*, 69. Also Shulman, June 22, 1991.

112. Shulman, *The Photography of Architecture and Design*, 69. Also, Stoller, interview, August 14, 1992; Rand, interview, August 24, 1992; Robinson, interview, January 22, 1993.

113. For more on this topic see Roland Barthes, *Image-Music-Text* (New York: Noonday Press, 1977); Roland Barthes, *Camera Lucida: Reflections on Photography* (New York: Noonday Press, 1981); David Freedberg, *The Power of Images: Studies in the History and Theory of Response* (Chicago: University of Chicago Press, 1989); Susan Sontag, *On Photography* (New York: Anchor Books, 1977); and Rosalind Krauss and Jane Livingston, *L'Amour Fou: Photography and Surrealism* (New York: Abbeville Press, 1985).

114. For more on the subject of duplication and reduplication in photography, see Craig Owens's insightful essay "Photography *en abyme*," reprinted in his collected essays, *Beyond Recognition: Representation, Power, and Culture*, eds. Scott Bryson et al. (Los Angeles: University of California Press, 1992).

115. Shulman, *The Photography of Architecture and Design*, 36.

116. Shulman, *The Photography of Architecture and Design*, 37.

117. Shulman, *The Photography of Architecture and Design*, 37.

118. Shulman, June 22, 1991, and October 24, 1991. Also, Shulman, *Photographing Architecture and Interiors*, 93, 96.

119. Shulman, June 22, 1991. Also, Shulman, *The Photography of Architecture and Design*, 52.

120. Shulman, June 18, 1991.

121. Flacke and Lindstrom, "Comments on Buildings," 8.

122. This occurred with the Neutra Kaufmann House in Palm Springs. The house was completed by 1947, but it was first published in the trade magazine *Architectural Forum* in June 1949 and in a consumer magazine, *Life*, in April 1949. The delay in publication came at the request of the owner. In a letter to Neutra, dated April 1, 1947, Henry Wright, the managing editor of *Architectural Forum*, states:

> When *Life* magazine checked directly with the Kaufmanns, their representative was told that they would prefer to defer publication of their house until the furnishing and landscaping were more complete.
>
> We are, of course, anxious to defer to their feelings in this matter, and both *Life* and *Forum* plan to hold off publication until then. . . . We have asked the Kaufmanns grant us exclusive publishing rights in the professional trade, to prevent premature publication elsewhere.

In a later letter to Neutra, dated June 17, 1947, Wright states: "We have also seen Julius Shulman, and have gone over again all of the pictures you showed us. . . . It seems desirable to all that a few of these pictures can be made over when the plantry has had a chance to develop further."

Shulman's Neutra client file cards list the house as having been photographed a total of three times: in 1947 (no month is specified), on March 1, 1949, and for The Museum of Modern Art in early 1965. His classic photograph of the house at twilight was produced in 1947; contrary to the correspondence between Wright and Neutra, the photograph was featured in a two-page spread for an article on Shulman's photography in *Life* on April 11, 1949. This 1947 photograph, however, was also featured in the premiere article on Neutra's Kaufmann House in *Architectural Forum* in June 1949. Shulman Archives; Wright to Neutra, April 1, 1947, and June 17, 1947, Neutra Collection; John Peter, "Glamourized Houses," *Life*, April 11, 1949, 146–48; "House in the Desert," *Architectural Forum*, June 1949, 90–95.

123.   Hines, *Richard Neutra and the Search*, 253; Shulman, June 22, 1991.

124.   Fisher, "Image Building," 92.

125.   Marylou Luther, "So You Want to be a Photographer? Know the Negative, Warns Professional," undated newspaper article, Shulman Archives.

126.   "Julius Shulman, Four Decades of Success," *Professional Photographer West*, January 1976, 1.

127.   "By making many reproductions it substitutes a plurality of copies for a unique existence. And in permitting the reproduction to meet the beholder or listener in his own particular situation, it reactivates the object reproduced." For more on the notion of aura, see Walter Benjamin, "The Work of Art in the Age of Mechanical Reproduction," in *Illuminations* (New York: Schocken Books, 1969), 221.

128.   Luther, "So You Want to be a Photographer?"

129.   Shulman, September 25, 1992.

130.   McCoy, "Persistence of Vision," 91; Cervin Robinson and Joel Herschmann, *Architecture Transformed: A History of the Photography of Buildings from 1839 to the Present* (Cambridge: MIT Press, 1987), 146.

131.   Julius Shulman, "Domestic Fidelity," *Architecture California*, May 1992, 31–32.

132.   See Lynn Spiegel, "Installing the Television Set: Popular Discourse on Television and Domestic Space, 1948–1955," *Camera Obscura* 16 (January 1988): 11–48; Judy Wajcman, *Feminism Confronts Technology* (University Park, Pa.: Pennsylvania State University Press, 1991), 87–95; and Stuart Ewen, *All Consuming Images: The Politics of Style in Contemporary Culture* (New York: Basic Books, 1988), 217–33.

133.   Shulman, October 31, 1992.

134.   Shulman, *Photographing Architecture and Interiors*, 55.

135.   Shulman, *Photographing Architecture and Interiors*, 130.

136.   Frey, interview, July 10, 1992; Killingsworth, interview, August 25, 1992; Koenig, interview, September 5, 1992.

137.   Shulman, March 15, 1991.

138.   See Richard Pare, *Photography and Architecture: 1839–1939* (Montreal: Canadian Centre for Architecture, 1982), 12; and Beaumont Newhall, *The History of Photography: 1859 to the Present* (New York: Museum of Modern Art, 1988), 23, 27, 48, 50, 59.

139.   Sean Callahan, ed., *The Photographs of Margaret Bourke-White* (New York: Bonanza Books, 1972), 205. In Bourke-White's memoirs, *Portrait of Myself* (New York: Simon & Schuster, 1963), she speaks at length of her first commissioned photo assignment, but the year is never mentioned: "On a red-glove day I got my first job. This was to photograph a new school, just finished, which had been designed by Pitkin & Mott, architects. . . . [They] were almost as new in their business as I was in mine, and therefore it meant a good deal to them to get their schoolhouse published in a national architectural magazine" (34). Furthermore, from 1927 to 1929, Bourke-White did more than ten commissioned shoots of domestic dwellings. These assignments are listed in the Bourke-White Papers by job title with a subtitle such as "estate," and usually a date; the names of the firms do not appear on the job list.

140.   "The building stood in the midst of a wasteland, littered with unused lumber, gravel dug out of the foundations, with withering remnants of workmen's lunches. . . . I ran to the nearest florist, invested in an armful of asters, carried them to the schoolhouse and stuck them in the muddy ground. Placing my camera low, I shot over the tops of the flowers, then moved my garden as I proceeded from one view-point to the next." Bourke-White, *Portrait of Myself*, 35.

141. "Between 1945 and 1949 he traveled throughout the New England and Middle Atlantic states. . . . In 1949 he was sent even farther afield, to Pittsburgh, Chicago, and various cities in Texas. . . . The number of Kertész photographs reproduced in *House & Garden* is astounding: more than 3,000 have been identified from the years 1945 to 1962, and the count is incomplete." Sandra S. Phillips, David Travis, and Weston J. Naef, *André Kertész: Of Paris and New York* (New York: Thames and Hudson, 1985), 117, 118. The East Coast–based architectural photographer Ezra Stoller also went on assignments for *House & Garden* at the time Kertész was under contract. In an interview on August 14, 1992, Stoller remembered, "Kertész was brilliant with black-and-white photography but not that good with color and many times I would be asked to reshoot his color assignments."

142. Nancy C. Barrett, *Ilse Bing: Three Decades of Photography* (New Orleans: New Orleans Museum of Art, 1985), 16. Bing's interest in photography began while she was a student of art history working on her dissertation proposal on Friedrich Gilly. She photographed Gilly's and Karl Friedrich Schinkel's work at this time. Ilse Bing, interview, July 7, 1992; the Ilse Bing Papers, Photographic Collection, Canadian Centre for Architecture, Montreal.

143. Pare, *Photography and Architecture*, 26, 269–70. Also, Robinson and Herschmann, *Architecture Transformed*, 113.

144. For more on Mantz, see *Werner Mantz Architekturphotographie in Köln 1926–1932* (Cologne: Museum Ludwig, 1982).

145. Robinson and Herschmann, *Architecture Transformed*, 113. Also, Ian Jeffrey, *Photography: A Concise History* (New York: Thames and Hudson, 1981), 7.

146. "Lucia Moholy almost always includes the surroundings in complete images, even if this obstructs the view. . . . If the groups of photographs are arranged appropriately, each building (workshop with offices and students' studio building, the masters' and Gropius' residence) is approached in a spiral [with] full panoramic views from all points of the compass." For more on Lucia Moholy, see Roland Sachsse's essay "Architectural and Product Photography," in *Photography at the Bauhaus*, ed. Jeannine Fiedler (Cambridge: MIT Press, 1990), 185–88. Also, Robinson and Herschmann, *Architecture Transformed*, 113.

147. Robinson and Herschmann, *Architecture Transformed*, 110.

148. Robert Elwall, "The Specialist Eye," in *Site Work: Architecture in Photography Since Early Modernism*, eds. Martin Caiger-Smith and David Chandler (London: Photographers' Gallery, 1991), 66. Interestingly, the architectural photographs by Frank Yerbury are omitted from this editorial swap of 1937. Yerbury was the predecessor of Dell and Wainwright in England. For a short time prior to Dell and Wainwrights's reign at the magazine, Yerbury was the official photographer of *Architectural Review*. For more on Yerbury, see Vicky Wilson, ed., *Frank Yerbury: Itinerant Cameraman, Architectural Photographs 1920–35*, (London: Architectural Association, 1987); on M. Oliver Dell and H. L. Wainwright, see Robinson and Herschmann, *Architecture Transformed*; on F. S. Lincoln, see Robinson and Herschmann, *Architecture Transformed*, and Pare, *Photography and Architecture*; on Ezra Stoller, see *Modern Architecture: Photography by Ezra Stoller*, with commentary by William S. Sanders (New York: Abrams, 1990); on Ken Hedrich of Hedrich-Blessing, see Robert A. Sobieszek, *The Architectural Photography of Hedrich-Blessing* (New York: Holt, Rinehart and Winston, 1984).

149. Paul Goldberger, "When Modernism Kissed the Land of Golden Dreams," *New York Times*, December 10, 1989.

150. Robinson and Herschmann, *Architecture Transformed*, 110.

151. "The architectural magazines . . . [are] inevitably contaminated by [an] 'aesthetic model' from advertising. . . . The published image must be able to strike the reader at first glance. The determinant in choosing what architecture to publish becomes the building's photogenic quality, a quality that is often totally independent of the real experience lived inside the building." For more on the role of image consumption in architectural periodicals, see Pierre-Alain Croset's insightful essay "Narration of Architecture," trans. Christian Hubert, in *Architectu-re-production*, ed. Joan Ockman (New York: Princeton Architectural Press, 1988), 203. For more on the issue of architectural photography in the twentieth century see, Akiko Busch, *The Photography of Architecture: Twelve Views* (New York: Van Nostrand Company, 1987); Joseph W. Moliter, *Architectural Photography* (New York: John Wiley & Sons, 1976); Rosemarie Haag Bletter, "Representing Architecture: The Drawings and the Photographs," *Architecture California*, May 1992; Jean-Louis Cohen, "The Misfortunes of the Image: Melnikov in Paris, 1925 (Architecture and Photography)," in *Architectu-re-production*; and Beatriz Colomina, "Le Corbusier and Photography," *Assemblage* 4 (1987).

PLATES
1930s–1980s

1930s 113

1940s 124

1950s 143

1960s 174

1970s 196

1980s 208

1

2

Plate 1
Smoke and Steam, 1934,
Los Angeles

Plate 2
L.A. Times Bombed, 1934,
Los Angeles

3

Plate 3
Fitzpatrick House, 1936,
Los Angeles,
R. M. Schindler, 1936

Plate 4
Lipetz House, 1936,
Los Angeles,
Raphael Soriano, 1936

Plate 5
Landfair Apartments, 1937,
Los Angeles,
Richard Neutra, 1937

4

5

6

Plate 6
Miller House, 1937,
Palm Springs,
Richard Neutra, 1937

Plate 7
Thomas Jefferson High
School, 1937,
Los Angeles, Morgan,
Walls and Clements, 1936

8

9

Plate 8
Wilshire Bus Stop, 1938,
Los Angeles

Plate 9
Sardi's Wilshire, 1938,
Los Angeles, ca. 1935

Plate 10
Terrace Theater, 1938,
Los Angeles, ca. 1935

Plate 11
Gas Station, 1938,
El Monte, ca. 1930

12

13

Plates 12, 13
Dunsmuir Apartments,
1938, Los Angeles,
Gregory Ain, 1937

Plates 14, 15
Apartments, 1939,
Los Angeles,
Milton J. Black, ca. 1935

14

15

17

Plate 16
I. Magnin & Company
Department Store, 1939,
Beverly Hills, *Myron Hunt
and H. C. Chambers, 1939*

Plate 17
Coulter's Department Store,
1939, Los Angeles,
Stiles O. Clements, 1937

19

20

Plates 18–20
Academy Theater, 1940,
Inglewood,
S. Charles Lee, 1939

125

21

22

Plates 21–23
Melchior House, 1941,
Los Angeles,
Frederick Monhoff, ca. 1940

24

Plate 24
Crenshaw Theater, 1942,
Los Angeles,
Paul Laszlo, ca. 1940

Plate 25
Pan Pacific Auditorium,
1942, Los Angeles,
Wurdeman and Becket, 1935

25

Plates 26, 27
Synthetics Factory (Dow
Chemical, Shell Oil, and
U.S. Rubber Co.), 1943,
Los Angeles

Plate 28
Prudential Building, 1949,
Los Angeles,
Wurdeman and Becket,
1948

27

28

29

30

31

32

Plates 29, 30
Joseph's Shoe Salon, 1947,
Beverly Hills,
Burton Schutt, ca. 1945

Plate 31
TWA Tourist Center, 1947,
Los Angeles,
Raymond Loewy, ca. 1945

Plate 32
American Lines Travel
Office, 1947, Los Angeles,
*Walter Dorwin Teague,
ca. 1945*

133

33

34

Plate 33
Palm Springs Tennis Club,
1947, Palm Springs,
A. Quincy Jones and Paul R.
Williams, 1947

Plate 34
Lockheed Ski Cabin, 1948,
Lake Arrowhead,
Lucille B. Raport, 1948

Plate 35
May Company Department
Store, 1948, Los Angeles,
A. C. Martin and S. A.
Marx, 1940

35

38

Plates 36, 37
Milliron's Department
Store, 1949, Los Angeles,
Gruen and Krummeck, 1949

Plate 38
Union Oil Gas Station,
1949, Pasadena,
Raymond Loewy, ca. 1947

39

40

41

Plate 39
Desert Hot Springs Motel,
1949, Desert Hot Springs,
John Lautner, 1947

Plate 40
Levin House, 1949,
Palm Springs,
William F. Cody, ca. 1945

Plate 41
Isley House, 1949,
Los Angeles,
Edla Muir, ca. 1945

43

44

Plate 42
Grossman House, 1949,
Los Angeles,
Greta Grossman, ca. 1945

Plates 43, 44
Engelberg House, 1949,
Los Angeles,
Harry Harrison, ca. 1945

46

Plate 45
Schutt House, 1949,
Los Angeles,
Burton Schutt, 1948

Plate 46
Millard House, 1950,
Pasadena,
Frank Lloyd Wright, 1923

Plate 47
Mutual Housing
Association, 1950,
Los Angeles,
Whitney R. Smith and A.
Quincy Jones with Edgardo
Contini, 1950

Plate 48
Downtown Los Angeles
from the Pasadena
Freeway, 1950

49

Plate 49
Tremaine House, 1950,
Montecito,
Richard Neutra, 1948

Plates 50, 51
Taliesin West, 1950,
near Scottsdale, Arizona,
Frank Lloyd Wright, 1942

Plates 52, 53
Ennis House, 1950,
Los Angeles,
Frank Lloyd Wright, 1924

53

54

55

56

57

Plates 54, 55
Davidson House, 1950,
Los Angeles,
J. R. Davidson, 1947

Plates 56, 57
Case Study House #9
(Entenza House), 1950,
Pacific Palisades,
Charles Eames and Eero
Saarinen, 1950

58

59

Plates 58, 59
Woods House, 1950,
Cave Creek, Arizona,
Paolo Soleri and Mark
Mills, 1949

Plate 60
Shulman House and Studio,
1950, Los Angeles,
Raphael Soriano, 1950

62

63

Plate 61
Stone House, 1951,
Beverly Hills,
J. R. Davidson, 1951

Plates 62, 63
Swedenborg Memorial
Chapel (Wayfarer's
Chapel), 1951,
Palos Verdes,
Lloyd Wright, 1949

64

65

66

67

Plates 64, 65
McKinney House, 1952,
Nabe Valley, New Mexico,
Mawn Associates, ca. 1950

Plate 66
Brody House, 1952,
Los Angeles,
*A. Quincy Jones, William
Haines (interiors), 1951*

Plate 67
Drake House, 1952,
Phoenix, Arizona,
Blaine Drake, ca. 1950

69

Plate 68
Moore House, 1952, Ojai,
Richard Neutra, 1952

Plate 69
Colby Apartments, 1952,
Los Angeles,
Raphael Soriano, 1952

159

70

Plate 70
Kramer House, 1953,
Norco,
Richard Neutra, 1953

Plate 71
Schindler and Chase
House, 1953,
West Hollywood,
R. M. Schindler, 1922

1950s

Plates 72, 73
Frey House I with additions,
1953, Palm Springs,
Clark & Frey, 1947, 1953

73

Plates 74–76
Freeman House, 1953,
Los Angeles,
Frank Lloyd Wright, 1924

74

75

77

78

Plate 77
Dodge House, 1954,
West Hollywood,
Irving Gill, 1916

Plate 78
Erlik House, 1954,
Hollywood,
R. M. Schindler, 1952

79

Plate 79
Chapel of the Holy Cross,
1956, Sedona, Arizona,
Anshen & Allen, 1956

Plate 80
Gemological Institute of
America, 1956,
Los Angeles,
Richard Neutra, 1955

81

Plate 81
Booth House, 1956,
Beverly Hills,
Smith & Williams, 1955

Plate 82
Steel Prototype House
(Jones House #2), 1956,
Los Angeles,
A. Quincy Jones, 1956

170

Plate 83
Stevens College Chapel,
1957, Columbia, Missouri,
Eero Saarinen, ca. 1955

Plate 84
Chuey House, 1958,
Los Angeles,
Richard Neutra, 1956

83

Plate 85
Singleton House, 1960,
Los Angeles,
Richard Neutra, 1959

86

87

88

Plate 86
Davis House, 1960,
Lake Arrowhead,
David Fowler, ca. 1960

Plates 87, 88
Bavinger House, 1960,
Norman, Oklahoma,
Bruce Goff, 1955

FOLLOWING PAGES
Plate 89
**Case Study House #23
(triad)**, 1960, La Jolla,
*Killingsworth, Brady and
Smith, 1960*

Plate 90
Jerome House, 1960,
La Jolla,
*Henry Hester, Gerald
Jerome (interiors), ca. 1955*

91

1960s

Plate 91
Parke-Davis Building, 1960,
Los Angeles,
Charles Luckman, ca. 1960

Plate 92
"Dome" House, 1962,
Los Angeles,
Bernard Judge, 1960

Plate 93
Pereira House, 1962,
Los Angeles,
William L. Pereira, ca. 1960

92

93

Plate 94
Duffield's Lincoln-Mercury
Showroom, 1963,
Long Beach,
*Killingsworth, Brady and
Smith, 1963*

Plate 95
St. Patrick's Church, 1963,
Tulsa, Oklahoma,
*Murray, Jones & Murray,
ca. 1960*

Plate 96
Community Church, 1963,
Garden Grove,
Richard Neutra, 1962

95

96

98

Plate 97
Marina City, 1963,
Chicago, Illinois,
Bertrand Goldberg, 1959

Plate 98
Kahala Hilton Hotel, 1964,
Honolulu, Hawaii,
*Killingsworth, Brady &
Associates, 1964*

99

100

101

Plate 99
Getty Estate, 1964, Sutton Place, Surrey, England

Plate 100
Alfred Newton Richards Medical Research Building, 1963, University of Pennsylvania, Philadephia, *Louis I. Kahn, 1960*

Plate 101
Rosen House, 1964, Los Angeles, *Craig Ellwood, 1962*

187

Plates 102, 103
Solomon R. Guggenheim
Museum, 1964,
New York, New York,
Frank Lloyd Wright, 1959

Plate 104
Parking Garage, 1965,
San Diego,
Tucker, Sadler & Bennet, 1965

102

103

105

Plate 105
Los Angeles Department of
Water and Power, 1965,
Los Angeles,
*A. C. Martin and Associates,
1964*

Plate 106
Frey House II, 1965,
*Palm Springs,
Albert Frey, 1964*

Plate 107
Case Study House #28,
1966, *Thousand Oaks,
Buff, Hensman & Associates,
1966*

FOLLOWING PAGES
Plate 108
Bank of London, 1967,
*Buenos Aires, Argentina,
Testa, Elia & Ramos,
ca. 1965*

Plate 109
Watts Towers, 1967,
*Los Angeles,
Simon Rodia, 1921–54*

106

107

110

111

1960s

Plate 110
Lovell Beach House, 1968,
Newport Beach,
R. M. Schindler, 1926

Plate 111
Chiat House, 1968,
South Pasadena,
Carl Maston, 1967

Plate 112
Bullock's Wilshire
Department Store, 1969,
Los Angeles,
*John and Donald Parkinson,
1928*

Plate 113
Bank of California, 1969,
San Francisco,
Anshen & Allen, 1968

112

113

195

114

115

Plates 114, 115
McNulty House, 1970,
Lincoln, Massachusetts,
*Mary Otis Stevens and
Thomas McNulty, 1965*

Plate 116
Wolff House, 1970,
Los Angeles,
John Lautner, 1961

FOLLOWING PAGES
Plate 117
Bradbury Building, 1970,
Los Angeles,
George H. Wyman, 1893

Plate 118
C. Y. Stephens Auditorium,
1970, Iowa State
University, Ames,
Crites & McConnell, ca. 1970

197

119

Plate 119
Pregerson House, 1971,
Santa Monica,
Kahn, Kappe, Lotery,
ca. 1970

Plate 120
Arango House, 1973,
Acapulco, Mexico,
John Lautner, 1973

Plate 121
Garcia House, 1975,
Los Angeles,
John Lautner, 1962

120

121

122

123

124

Plate 122
Saint Basil's Roman
Catholic Church, 1975,
Los Angeles,
A. C. Martin and Associates,
1974

Plate 123
Kittle House, 1976, Gaviota,
Zomeworks, Inc., 1975

Plate 124
Keystone Sky Resort, 1976,
Keystone, Colorado,
David Jay Flood, ca. 1975

125

Plates 125, 126
Barnsdall (Hollyhock)
House, 1977,
Los Angeles,
Frank Lloyd Wright, 1920

Plate 127
Samuel-Navarro House,
1978, Los Angeles,
Lloyd Wright, 1928

126

205

128

Plate 128
The Cathedral, 1977,
Brasilia, Brazil,
Oscar Niemeyer, 1959

Plate 129
Congress Building and
Ministries, 1977,
Brasilia, Brazil,
Oscar Niemeyer, 1958

130

131

Plates 130, 131
Reiner (Silvertop) House,
1980, Los Angeles,
John Lautner, 1963

Plate 132
Harder House, 1980, near
Mountain Lake, Minnesota,
Bruce Goff, 1979

133

134

Plate 133
Ocho Cascades, 1980,
Puerto Vallarta, Mexico,
Edward Giddings, ca. 1980

Plate 134
Buff House, 1980,
Pasadena,
Buff and Hensman, 1980

Plate 135
John Deere and Company,
Adminstration Center, 1981,
Moline, Illinois,
Eero Saarinen, 1963

Plate 136
Ehrlich House, 1981,
Los Angeles,
Steven Ehrlich, ca. 1980

135

136

211

137

Plate 137
Sporting Club, 1981,
Huixquilucan, Mexico,
Ricardo Legorreta, 1981

Plate 138
Rufino Tamayo Museum,
1981, Mexico City, Mexico,
*Abraham Zabludovsky with
Teodoro Gonzalez de Leon,
1981*

Plate 139
**Nissan International Design
Center,** 1983, La Jolla,
Ronchetti Associates, 1983

138

MY ODYSSEY

My photography preserves the work of those great pioneers of architectural history who have been too frequently denied by current generations of architects. A constant query in my mind during research of my archives has been, Why and how did I become involved with architecture? During my childhood I had no contact with photography or architecture. The only link that I can possibly identify seems to have been generated by my constant, close relationship with nature. For me, nature was orderly and so well disciplined that it appealed to my ingrained need for such characteristics. I remember that one of the earliest photographs I took with my vest-pocket Kodak was a detail of a bridge over the L.A. River in 1933 *(fig. 6, page 39)*. It earned a top award in a New York magazine; Margaret Bourke-White was the judge. During the following year, 1934, while at Berkeley, I was fascinated by the structural lines of a windswept tree on a hilltop. It had a curvilinear form that seemed to touch a "reverse" curve of a group of trees in the distance. That sixty-year-old composition is still one of my favorite architectural scenes *(fig. 5, page 37)*.

A revealing factor in most of my early photographs is my attraction to pattern and form in nature. Design was not my initial goal. My childhood on a farm in Connecticut, followed by years of close kinship with the outdoors when I was a Boy Scout, certainly indoctrinated me in nature's mysteries. This may indirectly have led to my participation in the massive "Project: Environment, U.S.A.," in 1964. Years later, after a conversation with Ansel Adams in Yosemite, the concept for a workshop on "The Architecture of Nature" was born; it was conducted in Yosemite after Adams's death in 1984.

A reverence for forms became constant in my work as my life became specifically interwoven with the design of forms, natural and architectural. The discipline of International Style architecture, as practiced by my first clients, directed me toward what may be called a severity of perception. My compositions of design were frequently those in which I adhered to a one-point perspective. Those scenes in particular delighted the most exacting architects, who appreciated the specific echoing of their drawings.

My life seems to have been full of curious architectural acquaintances. One that specifically comes to mind is *House Beautiful*'s architectural editor Elizabeth Gordon, who had conducted a campaign in the pages of the magazine condemning those architects whose work pursued the disciplined statements projected by Mies van der Rohe's philosophy "less is more." Gordon severely reprimanded the architects throughout the world who practiced "minimal" architecture. Her essays stated that this type of architecture would produce dissatisfaction among clients, who would be forced to accept compromising spaces and whose subsequent lifestyles would be molded so as to deliberately "incite Communism." I have often wondered why so few architects participate with the photographer in the recording of their designs. Architects were frequently prone to excuse their failure to accompany me on assignments by saying that I could comprehend their work so thoroughly that they need not be there. I never really accepted this as a compliment; on the contrary, I felt that they were lazy and perhaps indifferent, taking it for granted that I would produce fine images without their presence, saving them time away from their offices. Some of my most rewarding results were assignments created with the architect (or editor) on hand to view the 4 x 5 Polaroid exposure of the scene. I find that give-and-take sort of procedure frequently improves a composition. Richard Neutra put it succinctly: "After what involved as much as a year or two of planning, debating, discussion, and arguing with contractors, how rewarding to spend days with you, to study, to evaluate design statements, to scan the camera's ground glass, and finally to relax in bed on the evening of your delivery of the finished works. . . . The crisp, brilliant glossy prints—what a summation." To observe a space reduced to an 8 x 10 glossy offers a total, instant design review. The reduction in scale allows the architect a second look at his initial statement. When Neutra said "Even I could learn from photography," I was stunned, for Neutra had discouraged me from taking photographs without first letting him review the camera's imagery. But when, against his wishes, I produced the famous twilight photograph of his Kaufmann House in Palm Springs (one of my most requested images), it must have had some effect on his resistance.

There has been comparatively little illustration done by infrared photography and this seems a pity to me, for it is another technique that commands attention photographically. Its application in fields other than architecture could be highly successful in adding drama and information to black-and-white pages—particularly information, for purposes of delineating and of surmounting difficult atmospheric conditions.

A black-and-white photograph is an abstraction rather than a reproduction of subject matter. In its monochromatic state, it tends to emphasize form and tone at the expense of the total expression possible by color photography. Thus, if the purpose of the photograph is to illustrate the design statement of another artist, black and white becomes a highly communicative and honest way of doing so. Since this is frequently the purpose of an architectural photograph, the choice of black and white as a medium is dictated by its excellence in stressing line and mass, rather than by matters of economy. However, if black-and-white photography is to be dramatic and demanding of the attention it deserves, it requires a photographer's knowledge of and sympathy for subject matter. It also requires a certainty of technique and a feel for shapes and tones. It is at its best as a medium when it is given the respect which is its due. Good black and white does not happen as a quick, inexpensive substitute for color. I feel that too frequently color, albeit like a layer of salve, induces a veneerlike impact, thereby resulting in the often heard exclamation "What great color!" rather than a more genuinely desired response to form and design context.

I see my role as important in portraying images of architectural designs for the purpose of demonstrating the ultimate role of the designer in creating structures. The photographer must assume the responsibility of projecting that to the printed page; in turn we become archivists. The thought also occurs to me that our initial purpose of composition as architectural photographers is to introduce an almost purely objective exposure—that perhaps the "art" content was not even a consideration. Based on my experience, great rewards are felt by the photographer who allows a bit of imagination and experimentation to enter into the process before tripping the shutter. I have felt the greatest privilege: the freedom of expressing my reaction to the architect's production.

Finally, I feel that as an architectural photographer, I assume full responsibility. But I still contemplate the question posed to me in 1963 by Walter Gropius: "Does the photographer or the architect anticipate what is being resolved during an exposure?"

Julius Shulman
Los Angeles, 1992

215

SHULMAN CLIENT LIST

This list spans the fifty years of Shulman's professional career. The client list has been divided into three categories: architects and designers, companies and institutions, and publications. In each category only the name of the client appears without specific building lists or dates of photographs taken. The list of publications is comprised of magazines and newspapers that have commissoned Shulman to photograph assignments and does not reflect the vast number of magazines, newspapers, or books that have featured Shulman photographs over the last fifty years. The intent of this listing is to give an overview of the vast scope of Shulman's archives, rather than a detailed and all-inclusive listing.

Architects & Designers

A

Thornton Abell
Kazumi Adachi
Gregory Ain
Robert Alexander
Ralph Allen & Associates
William Allen
Allen, Knowles & Miller
Allison & Rible
Miguel Amato
Carl Anderson
Howard Anderson
Nash J. Anderson
Anderson & McConnell
Anshen & Allen
Aotani & Oka
Arbogast, Jones and Reed
The Architects' Collaborative (TAC)
Harris Armstrong
Art Ansoorian
Jane Ashley

B

Steven Baer
Bailey, Bozalis, Dickinson, Roloff
Richard Balch
Baldon & Galper
Edward Larrabee Barnes
Fred Bassetti
Lois Battram
William S. Becket
Welton Becket & Associates
Pietro Belluschi
Maria Bergson
Barry Berkus
Biby & Associates
Don Biles
Bissell Associates
Milton J. Black

William Blurock & Associates
  (also Ellerbroek Blurock & Associates)
Bobrow Thomas & Associates
Brown Healy Bock
Herbert J. Brownell
Jim Buckley
Buff and Hensman
Buff, Hensman & Associates
Buff, Straub, and Hensman
Bull, Field, Volkmann, Stockwell
Burke, Kober, Nicolais
Burrows, Allen & Knowles
  (also Gates, Wilson, Burrows)

C

Robert Calhoun
Cambridge Seven Associates
Carde, Killefer
Robert Carter
Caudill, Rowlett, Scott
Milton Caughey
H. C. Chambers
Robson Chambers
Jose Chappe
Jim Charlton
Alice Choate
Chris Choate
Eugene Choy
Mario Ciampi
John Porter Clark (see also Albert Frey)
Stiles O. Clements
  (also Morgan, Walls and Clements)
William F. Cody
Edgardo Contini
Cooke, Frost, Greer & Schmandt
Verna Cornelius
Ross W. Cortese
Coston, Frankfurt & Short
Coston, Wallace, Watson
Cottingham & Cook
Ben Covert
Stan Cowan
Robert T. Cox
Crane & Associates

Rowland Crawford
Theodore Criley
Criley & McDowell Associates
Ray Crites
Crites & McConnell

D

Davis Curtis
Daniel, Mann, Johnson & Mendenhall
Kenneth Darling
J. R. Davidson
Ben Deane
Juan Luis Diaz
Eladio Diestag
Richard H. Dodd
Dorius, Kermit & Associates
Richard Dorman
Dougherty & Dougherty
Blaine Drake
Gordon Drake
Henry Dreyfuss

E

Charles and Ray Eames
Eames & Saarinen
Thomas Echternach
Fritz Eden
Steven Ehrlich
Sidney Eisenshtat
Craig Ellwood
Benjamin Engel
Engelbracht, Rice and Griffen
Arthur Erickson Associates

F

Rick Farber
William Ficker
Edwin Fields
John Fisher
Maurice Fleishman
Flewelling & Moody
David Jay Flood
Fong & Associates

Fong, Preston, Jung Associates
William Foster
David Fowler
Paul T. Frankel
Albert Frey (also Clark & Frey; Clark, Frey
  & Chambers; Frey & Chambers)

G

John Howard Gambles
Garland & Hilles
David Gebhard
Frank O. Gehry
Edward Giddings
Irving Gill
Peter Gluck & Associates
Gerald Godfrey
Bruce Goff
Bertrand Goldberg
Lois Gottlieb
Carlton Granbery
Pauline Graves
Herb Greene
Greene and Greene
Grillias, Savage, Alves Associates
Walter Gropius
Greta Grossman
Victor Gruen Associates
Gruen and Krummeck

H

Rick Hacker
William Haines
Harwell H. Harris
Harry Harrison
William Harrison
Harrison & Abramovitz
Ralph Haver
Hellmuth, Obata & Kassabaum
Henry Hester
Hester & Jones
Hinsch-Kay Associates
Paul Sterling Hoag
Camilee Holland
Douglas Honnold
Frank L. Hope
Myron Hunt
Huygens & Tappe

J

Gerald Jerome
Bud Johnson
David Johnson
James A. Johnson
Ken Johnson
Philip Johnson
Johnson Burgee

Allen Johnston
A. Fay Jones
A. Quincy Jones
Jones & Emmons
Bernard Judge

K

Louis I. Kahn
Kahn, Kappe, Lotery
Kamnitzer & Marks
Kamnitzer, Cotton, Vreeland
Karl Kamrath
Kanner & Meyer
Raymond Kappe
Karmi & Rechter
Roy H. Kelley
William Kesling
Kest & Goldrich
Killingsworth, Brady and Smith
Killingsworth, Brady & Associates
Jim Kinoshita
Jonathan Kirsch
Kite & Overpeck
Pierre Koenig
Kohlmann, Eckman, Hukill
William Krisel
Krisel & Shapiro
Ernest Kump
Eugene Kupper

L

Thorton Ladd
Howard Lane
Thomas Lane
Langdon and Wilson
Anthony Langford
Robert Langslet
Lamont Langworthy
Gunther Lanson
Matthew Lapota
Gary Larson
Paul Laszlo
John Lautner
Mike Lavicoli
Charles Lawrence
Harlan Lee
S. Charles Lee
Ricardo Legorreta
Richard Leitch
Barbara Lenox
Frederick Liebhardt & Eugene Weston
  Associates
Raymond Loewy
Lorimer & Case
Charles Luckman
Alvin Lustig
Maynard Lyndon

M

McDaniel & Moffitt
Mackinlay, Winnacker & McNeil
Thomas McNulty
Julio Villar Marcos
A. C. Martin and Associates
S. A. Marx
Carl Maston
Mawn Associates
Cliff May
Bernard Maybeck
Ludwig Mies van der Rohe
Mark Mills
Adolfo Miralles
Frederick Monhoff
Charles Moore
Henry Moore
James Moore
Julia Morgan
Allyn Morris
Mosher & Drew
Mossler, Randall, Deasy, Doe
William Muchow Associates
Edla Muir
Desmond Muirhead
Dudley Murphy
Murray, Jones & Murray

N

Dale Naegle
Otto and Gertrud Natzler
Neptune & Thomas
Dione Neutra
Richard Neutra
Neutra & Alexander
Oscar Niemeyer
Nomland and Nomland

O

Oda & McCarty
Lynda Olsen
Vladimir Ossipoff
Oxley, Landau & Partners

P

Palmer & Krisel
John and Donald Parkinson
David Parry
Mario Paysse
I. M. Pei
Cesar Pelli
William L. Pereira
Pereira and Luckman
Perkins & Will
Perls & Associates
Robert Peters

Gomez Platera
Donald Polsky
Richard Poper
Antoine Predock
Bart Prince
Pulliam, Zimmerman & Matheus

R

Griswold Raetze
Raiser and Elrod
Ramey and Himes
Lucille B. Raport
Rasmussen Associates
Wallace Reid
Rex and Spaulding
Lutah Maria Riggs
Riley & Bissell
Harry Rinker
Pinto Risso
Al Robertshaw
Rochlin and Baran
Simon Rodia
Ronchetti Associates
Rossetti Assocates
Larry O. Rourke
Rowland and Associates
Rudi, Lee, Dreyer Associates
Paul Rudolph

S

Eero Saarinen
Sadler & Bennett
Uriel Schiller
R. M. Schindler
Burton Schutt
Schweiker & Elting
Harry Seidler
George Seminoff
Josep Lluis Sert
Abraham Shapiro
Sharon and Idelson
Shepley, Bulfinch, Richardson & Abbott
Daniel Simon
Skidmore, Owings & Merrill
Robert Skinner
Whitney R. Smith
Smith & Williams
Paolo Soleri
Raphael Soriano
William Stephenson
Mary Otis Stevens
Edmund Stevens
Stickney & Lewis
Edward Durrell Stone
Arthur Swab

T

Walter Dorwin Teague
Testa, Elia & Ramos
Tharp and Williams
Thorson, Brom, Broshar, Snyder, Inc.
Paul Thoryk
Tozier & Abbott
Tucker, Sadler & Bennet

V

Van Keppel and Green
Edward L. Varney

W

Rodney A. Walker
Harry Weese
Marc Weil
Albert Wein
White & Associates
Paul R. Williams
Stewart Williams
Williams & Williams
Adrian Wilson Associates
Zelma Wilson
Wittkower & Baumann
Marco Wolff
Don Woolf
Frank Lloyd Wright
Lloyd Wright
Wright and Selby
Wurdeman and Becket
Wurster and Bernardi
George H. Wyman

Y

Minoru Yamasaki

Z

Abraham Zabludovsky
Zigner & Associates
Eric Zimmerman
Milton Zolotow
Zomeworks, Inc.

Companies & Institutions

Aluminum Company of America
American Crayon Co.
American Institute of Architects
American Structural Products
American Wood Council
Armstrong Cork Co.
The Austin Company
Austrian Trade Delegation
Bechtel Corporation
Bethlehem Steel Corporation
Beverly Hilton Hotel
Beverly Realty
Bluffs Newport Beach
Bonaventure Hotel
Bren Investment Properties
Broadway Department Store
Bullock's Wilshire Department Store
California Council of Landscape
    Architects
California Federal Savings
California Redwood Associates
Cardoza Development Corp.
Carnation Products
CBS Television
Coldwell-Banker
Concrete Masonry Associates
C.I.T. Financial Corp.
Community Redevelopment Agency of
    Los Angeles
Countess Mara
Culters Department Store
Cultural Heritage Board, Los Angeles
Cummins Engine Co.
Cunningham & Walsh
Da Camera Society
Leo Daly Co.
Dempsey Construction Corp.
Douglas Fir Plywood Association
Elysian Park Committee
First National Realty &
    Construction Corp.
Frank Brothers
Golden State Mutual Life Insurance
Hanford Associates
Huntington Pacific Corporation
Inryco
Interbay Develoment Company
Interface Communications
Irvine Pacific Development
The Issac Group
Jewish Federation
Jewish Home for the Aged
The Koll Co.
Lever Brothers

L.A. Community Design Center
Los Angeles County Museum of
   Natural History
Los Angeles County Museum of Art
Los Angeles City Regional Planning
The Los Angeles Examiner
Los Angeles Municipal Art Department
The Los Angeles Times
McCarthy Co.
Macco Corporation
Merrill Lynch Realty
Meyer Investment Properties
Meyer, Kurt & Associates
Modern Color
Mulholland Regional Park Program
Museum of Modern Art, New York
The New York Times
Nissan
Orange County Masonry Associates
Owens Illinois Glass
Pan American Airlines
Pardee Construction Company
Penguin Books
Pittsburgh Plate Glass Company
Radiant Heat Engineering, Southern
   California Co.
Rodeo Realty
Rosebud Press
Sands Realty
Security Pacific Bank
Sheraton Hotels
Signal Investment Co.
Southern California Homes
Standard Oil of Indiana
Sunrise Corporation
Tishman Realty Construction
Toyota Corporation
Trans-Pacific Development Company
Tucker, Sadler & Bennett
Union Bank
Urban Innovation Group
U.S. Gypsum Company
Voit Corp.
Western Red Cedar Assocation
Westlake Village
Westward Construction Corp.
Woman's Architecture League

Publications

American Home
American Plywood Association
   Magazine
Architectural Digest
Architectural Forum
Architectural Record
Architectural Review
Architecture (formerly AIA Journal)
Architecture d'Aujourd'hui
Architecture + Urbanism (A+U)
Architecture West
Arts & Architecture
   (formerly California Arts & Architecture)
Bauen und Wohnen
Baumeister
Better Homes
Better Homes & Gardens
Brick and Tile
Building and Remodeling
Building Design & Construction
Building Progress
California Home
Celestial Arts
City
Colliers
Concrete Masonry Age
Connaissance des Arts
Designers West
Domus
Du
Epoca
Family Circle
Farm Journal
Fortune
Good Housekeeping
Harper's Bazaar
Holiday
Home Modernizing
House & Garden
House & Home
House Beautiful
Hvi
Industrial Photography
Interiors
Ladies' Home Journal
Librairie Larousse
Life
Living for Young Homemakers
Living Now
Look
Los Angeles Times Home Magazine
Los Angeles Magazine
McCalls
Masonry Industry

Medical Economics
Modern Hospital
New Homes Guide
New West
Orbit
Pacific Architect & Builder
Parents
Perfect Home
Photo Technique
Popular Home
Professional Builder
Professional Photographer
Progressive Architecture
   (formerly Pencil Points)
Redwood News
San Diego Magazine
Saturday Review
Schoner Wohnen
Sourcebook
Stern
Sunset
Time
Today's Home
Town & Country
Town Journal
Travelodge
United States Information Agency
Vogue
Women's Day

SELECTED BIBLIOGRAPHY

Writings by Shulman

"Angles in Architectural Photography." *AIA Journal,* March 1968, 53–60.

"The Architect and the Photographer." *AIA Journal,* December 1959, 41–44.

"Architecture and Historic Places." In *The Best of Los Angeles: A Discriminating Guide.* Los Angeles: Rosebud Books, 1980.

"Book Review—*Harwell Hamilton Harris,* by Lisa German." *L.A. Architect,* April 1992, 13.

"Building Images—A Close-up Look at Architectural Photography." *The Professional Photographer,* July 1979, 41–45.

"A Case for an Honest Awards Image." *AIA Journal,* August 1968, 59–63.

"Domestic Fidelity." *Architecture California,* May 1992, 31–34.

"An Emphasis on Shape." *Applied Photography.* No. 45. Rochester, N.Y.: Eastman Kodak Company, 1970, 10–17.

"The Format Connection." *Photomethods,* July 1985, 14–20.

"Integrity, Discipline and Elegance: Craig Ellwood." *L.A. Architect,* July/August 1992, 7.

"Julius Shulman on Architectural Photography." *Studio Light/Commercial Camera.* Vol. 2, no. 4. Rochester, N.Y.: Eastman Kodak Company, 1970.

"On Architectural Photography and the Work of R. M. Schindler." In *R. M. Schindler, Architect,* by August Sarnitz. New York: Rizzoli, 1988.

"A Photographer's Perspective on Neutra." *AIA Journal,* March 1977, 54–61.

Photographing Architecture and Interiors. New York: Whitney Library of Design, 1962.

"Photographing Interiors." *Interiors,* June 1962, 84–89.

The Photography of Architecture and Design. New York: Whitney Library of Design, 1977.

"Project: Environment, USA." *AIA Journal,* October 1965, 45–52.

Shulman has also been a photographic consultant to numerous books and guides:

Baldon, Cleo, and Ib Melchior. *Steps and Stairways.* New York: Rizzoli, 1989.

Gebhard, David, and Robert Winter. *A Guide to Architecture in Los Angeles & Southern California.* Santa Barbara, Calif.: Peregrine Smith, 1977.

———. *Architecture in Los Angeles: A Compleat Guide.* Santa Barbara, Calif.: Peregrine Smith, 1984.

Kaplan, Sam Hall. *LA Lost & Found: An Architectural History of Los Angeles.* New York: Crown Publishers, 1987.

Polyzoides, Stephenos, Roger Sherwood, and James Tice. *Courtyard Housing in Los Angeles: A Typological Analysis.* Berkeley: University of California Press, 1982. Reprint. New York: Princeton Architectural Press, 1992.

Writings on Shulman

"Architectural Photography, A Portfolio." *Iowa Architect,* May/June 1983, 10–19.

"Award-Winning Pictures Demonstrate Importance of Photography to Architects." *New York Times,* December 25, 1960.

Busch, Akiko. *The Photography of Architecture: Twelve Views.* New York: Van Nostrand Company, 1987.

Caiger-Smith, Martin, ed. *Site Work: Architecture in Photography Since Early Modernism.* London: Photographers' Gallery, 1991.

Deloffre, Claude. "California Dreaming: Photographie par Julius Shulman." *City,* October 1988, 82–85.

Eggers, Ron. "Julius Shulman: Designer of Architectural Photographs." *The Rangefinder,* September 1980, 55–58.

"Eye on the 20th Century: Photographer Julius Shulman Chronicles the Masters." *Cartouche,* Summer 1988, 16.

Fisher, Thomas. "Image Building." *Progressive Architecture,* August 1990, 88–98.

Flacke, Chris, and Kathy Lindstrom. "Comments on Buildings: An Interview with Julius Shulman." *Offramp,* Fall 1990, 2–9.

Goldberger, Paul. "When Modernism Kissed the Land of Golden Dreams." *New York Times,* December 10, 1989.

Hines, Thomas. S. *Richard Neutra and the Search for Modern Architecture.* New York: Oxford University Press, 1982.

———. "Julius Shulman in 40th Year." *L.A. Architect,* December 1976.

Huser, Mary Ann. "He Has Built a Career in Photography." *New York Daily News,* August 29, 1988.

Jackson, Neil. " Metal-frame Houses of the Modern Movement in Los Angeles." *Journal of the Society of Architectural Historians of Great Britain* 32 (1989): 159, 172.

"Julius Shulman" (interview). *L.A. Architect,* April 1990, 6.

"Julius Shulman, Four Decades of Success." *Professional Photographers West,* January 1976, 1.

"Julius Shulman: Looking Beyond the Photo to Find Beauty in Design." *Los Angeles Home and Garden Magazine,* July 1980, 36–40.

Kaplan, Sam Hall. "Building His Career Was a Snap." *Los Angeles Times,* September 11, 1985.

————. *LA Lost & Found: An Architectural History of Los Angeles.* New York: Crown Publishers, 1987.

————. "Missionary for Modern Architecture." *Los Angeles Times,* May 14, 1988.

Kinchen, David M. "Photographer Marks 70th Birthday—Julius Shulman Reflects on Career." *Los Angeles Times,* October 5, 1980.

————. "Photographer Snaps Best Poses of Architectural Designs." *Arizona Republic,* October 26, 1980.

"Library Design, Skirts Stir Photog's Comments." *Wichita Eagle,* May 29, 1967.

McCoy, Esther. "Persistence of Vision: The Encompassing Eye of Architectural Photographer Julius Shulman." *Angeles,* March 1990, 84–91, 133.

McHenry, Bob. "Comment." *Western Hotel-Motel News,* September 1973, 3, 13.

Mackley, Mona. "Rise from Ashes Needed." *Phoenix Gazette,* November 21, 1966.

McMasters, Dan. "Julius Shulman's Celebration of Architecture." *Los Angeles Times,* October 12, 1980.

Molitor, Joseph W. *Architectural Photography.* New York: John Wiley & Sons, 1976, 148.

Muchnic, Suzanne. "Bradbury Building, 98, Sits for Photographer, 80." *Los Angeles Times,* August 3, 1991.

Peter, John. "Glamourized Houses." *Life,* April 11, 1949, 146–48.

"Photographer is a Celebrity Himself." *Las Vegas Review,* October 12, 1980.

Robinson, Cervin, and Joel Herschmann. *Architecture Transformed: A History of the Photography of Buildings from 1839 to the Present.* Cambridge: MIT Press, 1987.

Seidenbaum, Art. "Architects Take Bow." *Los Angeles Times,* June 13, 1969.

"Shulman Honored." *L.A. Architect,* March 1987, 10.

Weaver, David. "Words and Pictures." *L.A. Architect,* April 1983, 4–5.

Webb, Michael. "Poetry in Steel." *Metropolis,* November 1989, 46–51.

————. "Real Homes for Real People." *L.A. Style,* September 1989, 176–81.

Whiteson, Leon. "Museum Exhibit Focuses on Case Study Home Era." *Los Angeles Times,* October 15, 1989.

Wholden, Rosalind G. "Henry Moore: Deukalion of Modern Sculptors." *Arts & Architecture,* January 1965, 23.

Wilson, William. "Shulman Work at Barnsdall." *Los Angeles Times,* March 17, 1969.

"The World of Julius Shulman." *Flightime,* July 1969, 9–12.

EXHIBITIONS

This list includes only those exhibitions that have focused on Shulman's career as a photographer and does not include the vast number of architectural exhibitions to which Shulman has contributed photographs.

"Julius Shulman." Broadway-Crenshaw, Los Angeles, California, May 15–20, 1949.

"A Quarter of a Century of Architectural Photography by Julius Shulman." Building Center Architectural Gallery, Los Angeles, California, December 3–30, 1961.

"Project: Environment, U.S.A." California Museum of Science and Industry, Los Angeles, California, July 14–August 4, 1964.

"One-Third of a Century: A Retrospective of the Photography of Julius Shulman." Municipal Art Gallery, Los Angeles, California, March 5–30, 1969.

"The Beginnings: A Julius Shulman Retrospective." University of California at Los Angeles Graduate School of Architecture and Urban Planning, Los Angeles, California, October 1986.

"Site Work: Architecture in Photography Since Early Modernism." The Photographers' Gallery, London, October-November 1991.

INDEX

All numbers refer to page numbers. Numbers in **bold** refer to illustrations. All buildings and other works are listed under the name of the architect, designer, or artist.

ILLUSTRATION CREDITS

All photographs, except those listed below, are by Julius Shulman from the Shulman Archives, Shulman Holder. Numbers refer to page numbers.

The Architectural Press, *Architects' Journal,* London, England: 100

Bauhaus-Archiv, Museum Für Gestaltung, Berlin, Germany: 99 top

Collection Centre Canadien d'Architecture/Canadian Centre for Architecture, Montreal: 98 bottom, 99 bottom

Collection Centre Canadien d'Architecture/Canadian Centre for Architecture, Montreal; Houk Friedman Gallery, New York; copyright Ilse Bing, New York: 98 top

Ken Hedrich/Hedrich-Blessing, courtesy Chicago Historical Society: 97 bottom

Joan Hix (from the Shulman Archives): 2

F. S. Lincoln Collection, Fred L. Pattee Library, The Pennsylvania State University Libraries, Pennsylvania: 101

Ezra Stoller/ESTO: 97 top

Unidentified photographer (from the Shulman Archives): 37 top right, 50 top and bottom, 84 top